Woman's Day Book of Sewing

HG

Paul Hamlyn
Sydney·London
New York·Toronto

Woman's Day Book of Sewing

Lorraine Kloppman

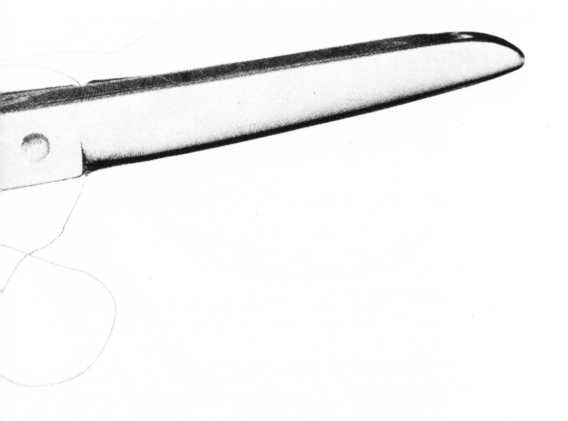

Published by Paul Hamlyn Pty Ltd
176 South Creek Road, Dee Why West, NSW 2099
First published 1973
Copyright Paul Hamlyn Pty Ltd 1973
Printed in Hong Kong
Designed by Catherine Higson
ISBN 0600 07120 0

Introduction

This is a book for the woman who sews—and for the woman who wants to sew. It describes in detail the many facets of sewing and shows you how to transform a piece of fabric into an attractive garment or a useful furnishing for your home.

Just knowing how to sew is not enough, however, for you must know how to select the right pattern for your figure, your personality and your way of life and then be able to fit and finish it so that it looks just like a top class ready-to-wear garment bought in a shop.

Likewise, to achieve that professional look with your home furnishings you must be able to choose fabrics correctly to suit their proposed use—for instance choosing light thin material for chair covers is a waste of time; and material for curtains should be guaranteed fadeless—and to suit the desired mood or personality of your home or of a particular room. Then having chosen your material you must know how to make it into a finished item worthy of display in any home.

This book has been planned to help you do all these things. It takes you step by step through the selection of styles, choice of fabrics and into their final making. Even the raw beginner will be able to turn out a professional-looking garment or furnishing.

Sewing can be fun. And as well it can be a pleasant, satisfying hobby, added to which is the enjoyment of wearing or using the results of your work.

Metric Guide

The tex has become the Australian standard unit for measuring the linear density of textiles. The new unit is described in Australian Standard 1128 Preferred Metric Units for Textiles, recently published by the Standards Association of Australia.

The standard provides a list of metric units to be used in the textile industry for the preparation of standards and for general commercial use. It will be of use in the preparation of company standards and trade literature and for the training of personnel so that a rational uniform system of units is used throughout the industry.

The standard includes multiples and sub-multiples of the units. For example, tex divided by 10 is decitex and multiplied by 1000 is kilotex.

CLOTHING AND TEXTILES

The centimetre is the common consumer unit of measurement for the description of clothing sizes, manchester sizes, fabric widths, etc. Traditional fabric widths will not change greatly on conversion.

Examples: As 1in is 2.5cm, a man's singlet previously sized as 40in will now be 102cm and a 36in width dress material will be 91cm. In women's clothing sizes numeric sizes such as Size 12 for a woman with inch measurements of 34 x 25½ x 36 will not change on conversion. Only the body measurements will change to centimetres, viz. (87 x 65 x 91). Similar changes will occur in children's and men's wear.

Piecegoods such as furnishing fabrics, dress and curtain materials are being sold by the metre which is 10 percent more than a yard, and tenths of a metre.

Bed and table linen is described in rounded metric units (centimetres) and there is little variation from the original sizes.

Metric knitting, crochet and dress patterns are now in use, but in most cases, both imperial and metric sizes are given, although in time new pattern books will be published only in metric units. Don't throw away your old patterns, for the only adjustment needed is in the amount of material expressed in metric units to be purchased to make up the pattern.

The gauge number of sewing threads is not changing and neither is the ply rating of wool. However, balls and skeins of knitting wool are 25 g (gram) instead of 1 oz (ounce), which is about 12 percent less, so that a pattern requiring 15 one oz balls will need 17, 25 g balls.

Contents

Part 1

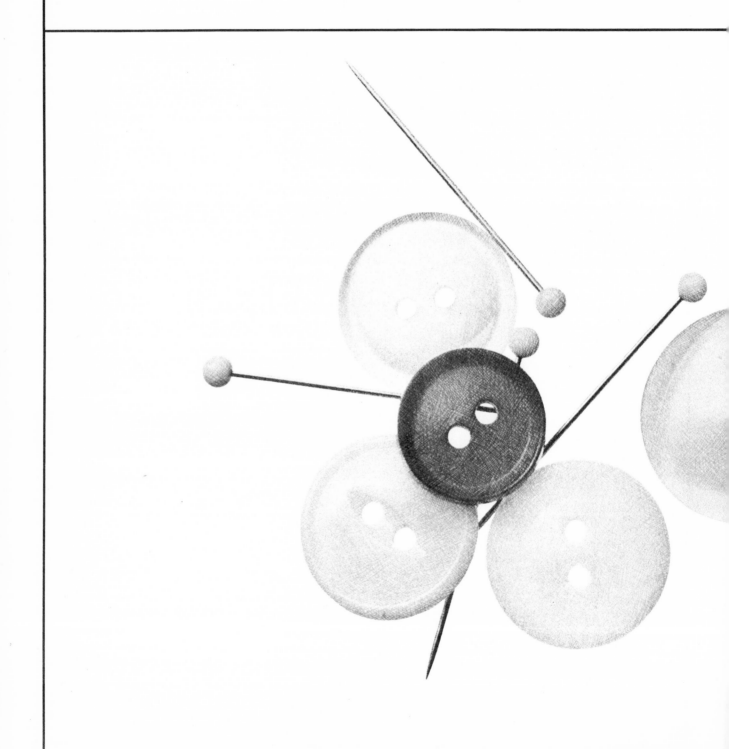

Keystone to Fashion

Individuality is the key to fashion today. The woman who sews can plan her own wardrobe with up-to-the-minute fashions to suit her figure and her personality. It is easy to teach yourself to sew. Begin with something simple and your efforts are rewarded from the start.

We have prepared this step-by-step guide to show you how to make your own garments and to add those finishing touches that make today's fashions so exciting.

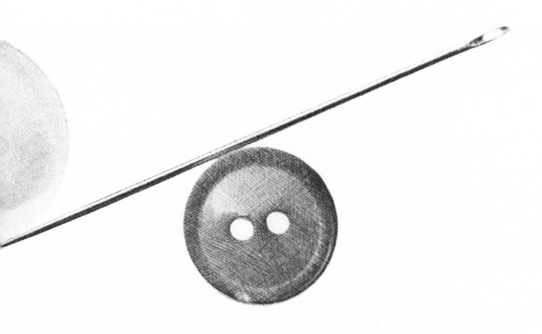

A Personal Measurement Chart

IF you plan to be your own dressmaker, it will be so much easier if you know your figure and pattern type.

It is a good idea to take measurements before buying each pattern. Figures can change, especially if you lose or gain weight easily, and you may need a different size and type of pattern from one you bought earlier.

It is necessary to take certain measurements and these are shown in diagram A. Those numbered 1, 2, 3, 4, are the body measurements on which your pattern type and size are based. Record all your measurements on the chart on page 11. When you start on your first project, shop for your pattern design using your newly taken bust, waist and hip measurements.

The back waist length measurement is the clue to your figure type; the bust measurement is the key to your correct size for all garments except skirts, slacks and shorts, for these garments buy by waist measurement. You should buy the same size pattern for a coat or jacket as for a dress or blouse.

When a pattern includes more than one type of garment, such as a wardrobe pattern or top and pants pattern, purchase by bust measurement. If bust and hip measurements require two different sizes, pattern alterations are easier to make in the hip area.

For skirt and pants patterns, buy the size shown on the measurement chart according to your waist measurement unless your hip measurement is larger than shown for that size. In that case, select size by hip measurement and adjust the waistline.

Pay heed to a pattern envelope. It has a wealth of important information. In addition to sizing facts it tells you what type of fabric is suitable and how much to buy, and all the extras you'll need, so that you'll be able to get everything in one trip.

Some tools you should invest in at this point are good, sharp dressmakers' shears, dressmakers' pins, tracing carbon and tracing wheel (for marking darts).

If this is to be your first sewing project you'll find firmly woven cottons or blends the easiest fabrics to work with.

Allow yourself plenty of space in which to work, with a big cleared table for cutting out on. You may find that the floor, covered with an old clean sheet, is more convenient.

A sewing time-saver: If you must make a good dress in a hurry, look for a pattern with few design details. Patterns such as Simplicity Jiffy are designed for quick and easy sewing, with a limited number of pieces.

Choose a fabric that doesn't need an underlining, a style which has facings as opposed to bindings or fancy collars that may require handwork. Look for raglan or kimono sleeves.

Avoid handwork wherever possible. Pin-baste, sparingly at the notches. Do as much work as you can by machine while the dress is still in its flat stage. Sew pockets and trims to the front. Put slide fasteners and any trims to the back, then join front to back.

Modern sewing machines make home sewing easy. One of the newest models saves lots of hand-sewing with its chain-stitch tacking that pulls out invisibly after fitting. It also makes buttonholes easier than ever—a special cam makes buttonholes any size with perfect stitch width and spacing.

10

1. BUST (around fullest part, tape slightly raised over shoulder blades)	
2. WAIST (comfortably, at natural waistline)	
3. HIPS (8in below natural waistline)	
4. BACK NECK TO WAIST (from prominent bone at back neck base to waistline)	
5. SHOULDER TO BUST (from neck base at shoulder to bust point. This is to find the correct location of the underarm dart)	
6. FRONT WAIST LENGTH (from back of neck over fullest part of bust to waistline)	
7. SLEEVE LENGTH a. Shoulder to Elbow (take with arm bent for correct location of sleeve darts) **b. Elbow to wrist** (take with arm bent for correct location of sleeve darts)	
8. BACKSKIRT LENGTH (from waistline to bottom of skirt down centre back)	

HOW TO TAKE
YOUR MEASUREMENTS

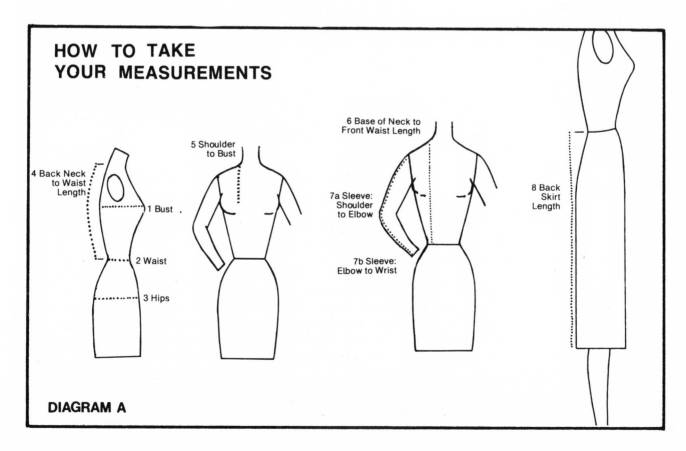

DIAGRAM A

11

Make Your Pattern a Personal Fit

PERFECT fit in a garment means personal fit. After you've taken accurate body measurements, the next step is to compare your dimensions with the pattern's 'body' measurement, and then to adjust the pattern accordingly.

A proper fitting bodice, be it dress, tunic or blouse, means darts pointing to the fullest part of the bust, comfortable sleeves, and an absence of unsightly wrinkles and pulls. Enter your measurements on the chart (right), then the measurements stated on the pattern. The difference between the two figures is the amount you must adjust.

How to adjust

If your pattern style has no waistline seam you will find the waistline indicated at the centre back. Draw a line at right angles to the centre back across to the side seams. Do the same for the front pattern piece at the waist. Diagrams 1 and 2 show you how to mark your pattern clearly to correspond with the measurements taken on your own body.

Using the figures in the adjust column, make any needed alterations in this order: shoulder length, back width, back waist length, front waist length, waist, hips, sleeve length. Reposition darts if necessary.

No garment fits as snugly as the tape measure. There is some ease or 'squirming room' added to every pattern to ensure wearing comfort, and some patterns include additional ease for fashion effects. To preserve the style, refer to the measurement chart and the differences between yours and the patterns 'body' for any adjustments needed.

To narrow shoulders: Just above armhole notch, clip pattern to seam line. From midpoint of shoulder seam, cut to armhole seam just above the pin. Place paper beneath and lap cut edges the needed amount. Fasten to paper. Draw new shoulder line as shown by broken line (diag 3).

To widen shoulders: Just above armhole notch, pin pattern to seam line. From midpoint of shoulder seam, slash to armhole seam slightly above pin. Spread pattern over paper to needed amount. Fasten. Draw a new cutting line as shown by broken line (diag 4).

To shorten back: At centre back bodice, measure up from waistline amount needed to shorten. Do the same at the centre of the waistline dart. Draw a line between these two marks. Taper it to nothing at the sides (diag 5).

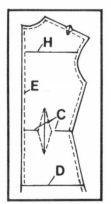

DIAGRAM 1

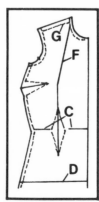

DIAGRAM 2

DIAGRAM 3

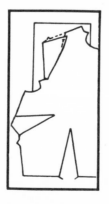

DIAGRAM 4

DIAGRAM 5

DIAGRAM 6

MEASUREMENTS	MINE	PATTERN	ADJUST
(a) bust			
(b) high bust			
(c) waist			
(d) hips			
(e) back waist length			
(f) front waist length			
(g) shoulder length			
(h) back width			
(i) sleeve length			

To lengthen back: At centre back bodice, measure down amount needed to lengthen. Draw a line. Extend darts to drawn line (diag 6).

To shorten sleeve: Measure up from the shortening line on the pattern the needed amount. (Above and/or below, as needed. Centre dart of three should come at the elbow.) Draw line. Fold pattern on shortening line. Bring fold up to drawn line and fasten. Draw new cutting line (diag 7).

To lengthen sleeve: Cut pattern apart on lengthening line (one above, one below elbow), place paper under the pieces. Spread pattern to wanted length. Draw new cutting line (diag 8).

To adjust waist: For a small increase, add adjustment to side seams (diag 9). For a large increase, add to side seams and make darts smaller (diag 10).

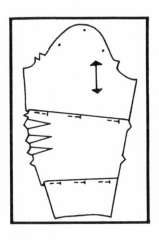

DIAGRAM 7

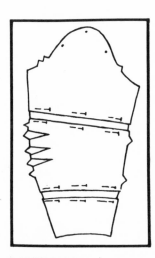

DIAGRAM 8

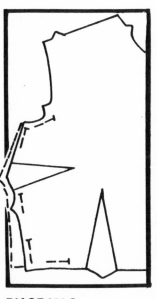

DIAGRAM 9

DIAGRAM 10

Basically simple designs can be turned into eye-catching outfits.

For a small decrease in waist, take in on side seams (diag 11). For a large decrease, take in on side seams and make darts larger (diag 12).

To widen hipline: At side seams of front and back, add ¼ the needed amount from waist to lower edge. To restore original waist, increase width of darts nearer the side seams the same amount added at side (diag 13).

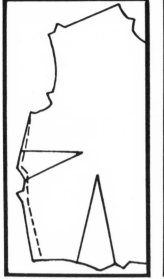 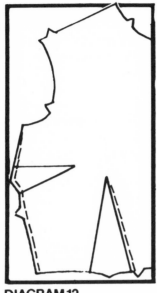

DIAGRAM 11 **DIAGRAM 12**

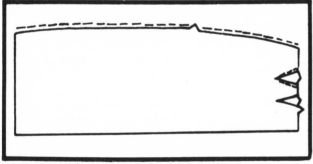

DIAGRAM 13

How to fit pants
How closely pants fit is mostly a personal matter, but always consider the activities for which the pants will be worn.

For accuracy of measurements you'll need an unstretchable tape measure and some string. Wear normal undergarments and tie the string snugly around your waist. Place your measurements in the inches column of the chart on page 16.

How to measure hips: Around body, at fullest area (diag 14, fig 1).

Crotch depth: Sit on a hard chair, feet flat on the floor (very important) and measure from waist to chair (diag 14, fig 2).

Waist to knee; knee to ankle-bone: Along outside of one leg (diag 14, fig 1).

Crotch seam: Run tape measure from waist in back, between legs, to waist in front (diag 14, fig 3).

Front crotch length: With tape in same position as for crotch seam, measure from waist string in front to a spot in the centre of inside leg, as close to body as possible.

Back crotch length: Subtract front crotch length from crotch seam measurement.

Waist: Around natural waistline, snug enough to get one finger underneath (diag 14, fig 1).

Thigh girth; knee girth: Around leg at fullest part of thigh and knee (diag 14, fig 1).

Fill out the 'totals' column on the chart by adding the 'inches' and the 'minimum ease' columns. For crotch depth, add ½in ease if the hips are 36in or less, 1in if hips are 38in or more.

The 'totals' column now gives you the minimum measurements for your pants pattern at each of these points.

Purchase the pattern closest to your hip measurement.

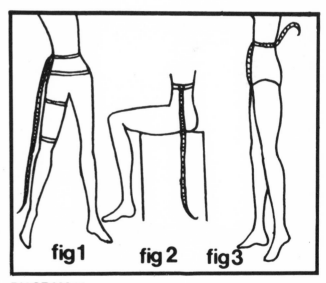

fig 1 **fig 2** **fig 3**

DIAGRAM 14

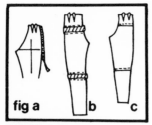

DIAGRAM 15

To adjust pattern

Open out your pattern and draw a line, if not already on your pattern, from the crotch point at inside seam, at right angles to the grain line, to side seam (diag 15,a). This line should be indicated on both front and back main pattern pieces.

The pattern crotch depth is measured from this line where it meets side seam to waist seam (diag 15,a). Compare this to your crotch depth marked on the chart.

Adjust length from waist to knee, or knee to ankle, by inserting paper strips to lengthen (diag 15,b) or making tucks to shorten (diag 15,c). Make identical alterations on front and back pattern pieces.

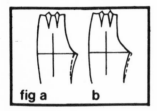

DIAGRAM 16

Next adjust both back and front crotch lengths to measurements in 'totals' column. To shorten crotch, see diag 16,a. To lengthen crotch, see diag 16,b.

If your waist is smaller than the pattern measurement, divide the difference by the number of darts back and front and make each dart larger by this amount. If your waist is larger, decrease darts by the same method, or eliminate a dart on each side.

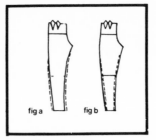

DIAGRAM 17

Adjust thigh or knee girth by adding width on leg side seams front and back (diag 17,a) or subtracting width on the leg side seams front and back (diag 17,b).

Avoid baggy-seated pants by pinning waistband around you before stitching it to the pants. Pin the pants to the band, raising or lowering them until you get a smooth professional 'hang'.

When you have them looking right, check for sitting comfort, adjust them if necessary, and stitch them up.

Much of the style in pants today is located below the knee, where the pants flare or not. Sometimes the flare is subtle. To help you predict just how your pants will look when made, measure the width of the leg at the hem (both pattern pieces). Straight pants will be 17in to 21in, more than 28in is a prominent flare, anything in between is considered a moderately-flared pants leg style.

How to fit gauchos

Gauchos are really midi-length pant-skirts. They begin their fullness at about the thigh area and are reminiscent of South American cowboys' gear.

Fitting them is no problem, once you've mastered pants. Use the same methods for measuring and altering pants at the waist, crotch and hip, and you'll be pleased every time.

Making a jumpsuit fit

Jumpsuits are the now and future fashion, and in

MEASUREMENTS	INCHES	MINIMUM EASE	TOTALS
hips		+2in	
crotch depth		+½in-1in	
waist to knee		none	
knee to anklebone		none	
crotch seam		+1½in	
back crotch length		+1in	
front crotch length		+½in	
waist		none	
thigh girth		+2in	
knee girth		+2in	

Well-cut clothes have beauty of line and require little superficial decoration to add to their charm, as shown with this pants suit and the gauchos.

Fabrics: Cotton, the most widely used of all the world's fibres **(A)**; checks **(B)**; knits, jerseys and tricots (warp or flat knits). **(C)**; nap and pile fabrics **(D)**; silk **(E)**; Stretch fabric **(F)**.

A

B

C

D

E

F

order to be the most flattering and comfortable they must fit you to a T—from your shoulders through your waist and crotch, down to your ankles. None of us is perfect, so our shoulders, waist and crotch don't always fall just where the pattern dictates they should. That can be remedied, however. Here's how you should go about it.

To start, buy the jumpsuit pattern by your bust measurement. Then take the following measurements and enter them on the chart below, after tying a string tightly around your middle to pinpoint your waistline: back waist from highest prominent neck bone to waist as in diag 18, fig 2 (A); crotch depth as in diag 18, fig 1 (B); front and back crotch, as in diag 18, fig 2 (C and D); hip at the fullest point (diag 18, fig 2, E), and waist to ankle (diag 18, fig 2, F).

For B, sit on a hard chair and measure from the string around your waist to the chair. Add ½in ease for figures with 36in hips or less, 1in for figures 37in or over through the hips. To determine C and D, measure your crotch from front waist to back waist, between your legs. This is the total crotch measurement. Then measure from your waist in front to a point between your legs, close to the torso, where you want the inside leg seam. This is measurement C. Subtract this from the total crotch measurement for D. Add 1in ease to C, 2in ease to D. When you have completed these measurements, record them. Now you're ready to adjust the pattern pieces.

Body measurements are given on the pattern envelope and ease is included for each particular style. Check your measurements for A, E and F and make necessary adjustments at 1, 5 and 6.

Once you've gone through this process your next jumpsuit will be easy to alter.

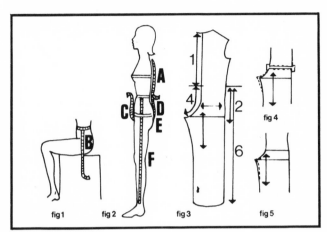

DIAGRAM 18

		INCHES	EASE
1 Back waist	A		
2 Crotch depth	B		½in to 1in
3 Front crotch	C		1in
4 Back crotch	D		2in
5 Hip	E		
6 Waist to ankle	F		

On the front and back pattern pieces, mark the crotch depth by drawing a line from the crotch points to the side seams, at right angles to the grain lines (diag 18, fig 3). Mark the waistline in this manner also. Measure the pattern from the waist to crotch as side seams (2). Check 2 against B (your measurement plus ease) and adjust the pattern accordingly, as shown in diag 18, figs 4 and 5. Compare C to 3 (front crotch seam, not shown here, as only back pattern pieces are illustrated) and D to 4, and lengthen or shorten the crotch seam lines, tapering the new inside leg seams (diag 18, figs 4 and 5).

Sewing Terms— What They Mean

SPECIAL terms are often used in directions for making up a garment. Some apply to fabrics and the way to cut them, others apply to methods of sewing. It is a help to know what they mean.

Selvage: The narrow, woven edge on lengthwise sides of a fabric (diag 1).

Grain: The direction of the threads of a fabric.
Lengthwise Grain: The threads that run up and down the fabric parallel to the selvage (diag 1).
Crosswise Grain: The threads that run across the fabric from selvage to selvage (diag 1).

Nap: 'With nap' refers to fabrics such as corduroy, velveteen, satin and fleece and to fabrics with a one-way design. These require a special cutting layout with all pattern pieces laid so their tops point in the same direction (diag 3).
'Without nap' pattern pieces can be placed either direction on fabric.

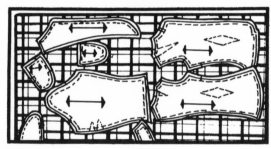

DIAGRAM 3

Basting: Is used to hold two or more pieces of fabric together temporarily until they are permanently stitched.
Pin-Basting: Holding fabric together by pins. Use enough pins to keep two layers of fabric from slipping. Place pins at right angles to edge and on seamline. Remove as you stitch, if you wish.
Hand-Basting: To sew temporarily by hand with long even, uneven or diagonal stitches (diag 4).
Machine-Basting: To sew temporarily by machine using the longest stitch. Useful for fitting garments. Before removing, clip thread every few inches and pull out bottom thread.

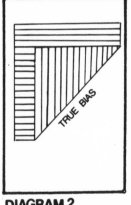

DIAGRAM 1 **DIAGRAM 2**

On Grain: A fabric is 'on grain' when lengthwise and crosswise threads run perpendicular to each other.

Off Grain: A fabric is 'off grain' when crosswise threads are not at right angles to selvage edge and fold.

Bias: Any direction away from the straight lengthwise or crosswise grain.
True Bias: The diagonal line formed when a fabric is folded so crosswise threads run in the same direction as the lengthwise threads (diag 2).

Baste-Stitch or Baste-Mark: To machine-baste as described above when there are construction details marked on the wrong side that are needed on the right side, such as buttonhole locations. Baste-stitch on the wrong side over the markings using contrast thread and the stitches can be seen on the right side.

Regular Stitching: This refers to the length of the machine stitch used in stitching your garment. About 12 stitches to the inch is the usual length. Try different lengths on a scrap of your fabric as stitch length may have to be varied.

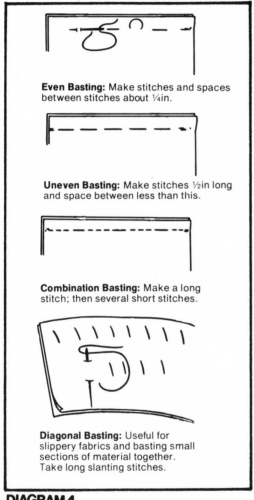

Even Basting: Make stitches and spaces between stitches about ¼in.

Uneven Basting: Make stitches ½in long and space between less than this.

Combination Basting: Make a long stitch; then several short stitches.

Diagonal Basting: Useful for slippery fabrics and basting small sections of material together. Take long slanting stitches.

DIAGRAM 4

Stay-Stitching: A line of stitching done on bias or curved edges that are to be joined to another piece. Stitch on a single thickness of material, ½in from the edge. (On deep curves, such as necklines, stay-stitch on the seam line, ⅝in from the edge.) Stay-stitching holds the grain so the fabric does not stretch in handling.

Backstitching: This stitching is used to secure thread ends. At the beginning of a line of stitching, place the needle in the fabric about ¼in from the edge and stitch backwards to the edge; then stitch forward. At the end of a stitching line, stitch backwards for about ¼in (diag 5). If your machine does not reverse stitch, leave the needle in the fabric at the end of the stitching; lift the presser foot and turn the fabric around on the needle. Lower the presser foot; stitch over the first stitching.

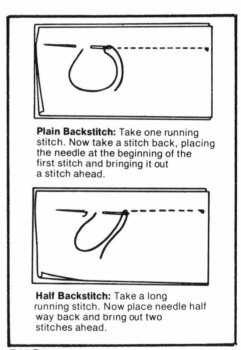

Plain Backstitch: Take one running stitch. Now take a stitch back, placing the needle at the beginning of the first stitch and bringing it out a stitch ahead.

Half Backstitch: Take a long running stitch. Now place needle half way back and bring out two stitches ahead.

DIAGRAM 5

Topstitching: Stitching made on the outside of a tailored garment close to a seam line, or for a decorative effect ¼in or more from an edge.

Gathering: Is to control fullness by drawing up fabric on a line of stitches. Use a medium long machine stitch and stitch on seam line. Place a second row ¼in from the first within seam allowance. For heavy fabrics such as corduroy or velveteen, hand-gather using stitches ¼in long (diag 6).

Slip-Stitching: An invisible hand-sewing for finishing hems or facings, and for joining edges of an opening. On hems or facings, pick up one

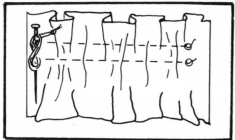

DIAGRAM 6

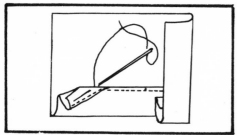

DIAGRAM 7

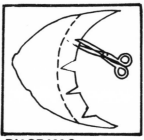

DIAGRAM 9

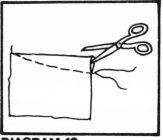

DIAGRAM 10

clipping, make a row of machine stitching on the seam line to strengthen it (diag 9).

Slash: On heavy fabric a curved dart is 'slashed' open through the fold edge after stitching so it will lie flat. The opening in a long sleeve is 'slashed' between the stitching lines (diag 10).

Trim: Reduces bulk of fabric. Trim a seam to make it narrower. You 'trim' a corner to remove the

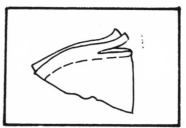

DIAGRAM 11

fabric that would bunch into the point when it is turned (diag 11). (Do not confuse this with 'trim' meaning to decorate!)

thread in under fabric. Take ⅛in stitch through fold of top fabric. To join edges, slip needle in fold of one edge, then in the other (diag 7).

Whip-Stitching: Used to join two pieces of fabric together, such as belts where stitches need to be invisible. Hold the edges of two pieces of ribbon together or the belt fabric and its lining. Turn both fabrics to the right side and stitch as shown (diag 8).

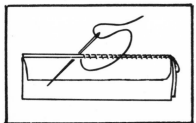

DIAGRAM 8

Eased seam: Extra length in one seam edge not found in the edge to which it is to be joined. The back shoulder seam is often slightly longer than the front shoulder seam.
To Ease In: Matching the longer seam to the shorter without gathers or puckers.
Ease-Stitching: Rows of stitching of about 12 stitches to the inch used to control the ease when there is more than just 'slight' fullness, such as at the top of sleeves. Put one row on the seam line and the other in about ¼in from the first within the seam allowance. Draw up the threads from both ends to distribute the fullness evenly.

Clip: To cut into the seam allowance from edge to seam line. 'Clip' a seam to spread outer edges to fit another section of the garment, or so a curved seam on neckline or collar will lie flat. Before

DIAGRAM 12

Grade: To trim seam allowances in different widths to reduce the bulk and give a flatter, smoother look (diag 12).

Tack: To hand-sew one section of a garment to another with a few loose stitches. For finish, you 'tack' a neckline facing to the garment at the shoulder seams (diag 13).

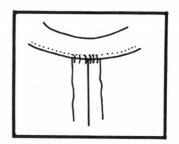

DIAGRAM 13

There is a variety of collar designs and trims to give a garment its individuality.

Know Your Fabrics and Finishes

THE right fabric can make all the difference to a garment and it can do wonders for your figure. Spend a little time in choosing the fabric for your next piece of sewing.

Fabrics are made from yarns: yarns are spun from fibres. Fibres used for fashion fabrics are natural (animal and vegetable) or man-made.

Among natural fibres there are:

Cotton: A vegetable fibre from seed pod of cotton plant, and it may be long or short staple.
Linen: The vegetable fibre from the flax plant.
Silk: Natural animal fibre from cocoon spun by the silk worm.
Wool: Natural animal fibre from the fleece of sheep or lamb. Also included in the wool 'family' are alpaca and angora goat fleeces and camel and llama hair, as well as vicuna, cashmere and mohair.

Man-made fibres come in two groups:

Cellulose Group: Includes rayon, acetate and triacetate. Processed from the natural fibrous sections of wood pulp. Although they have a natural base, chemistry is used to produce the fibres.
Synthetic Group: Term used generally for all man-made fibres, but it includes only the fibres that are chemically created, such as nylon, polyester, acrylic and many others.

Fabric Terms

BLEND: A yarn or fabric that combines the best qualities of two or more fibres, natural or man-made.

BONDED: (1) Non-woven fabrics made by pressing fibres together with a special bonding solution to hold the fibres together. (2) The term is applied to a single piece of fabric made by sealing two fabrics together, back-to-back, with a bonding agent of resin or glue. Fabric-to-fabric bonding is done for various reasons. Often woven and knit fabrics or laces are bonded to tricot knit or taffeta for self-lining; coating fabrics are bonded to interlining to retain shape; two face fabrics are bonded to make them reversible or with a layer of filling for extra warmth; open weaves to cotton backing for easy handling.

BOUCLE: Any fabric made from irregularly twisted yarns; woven or knitted to give a nobbly, uneven surface texture.

COARSE/ROUGH: Fabrics in this grouping are generally made of very thick and uneven yarns, or a combination of bulky yarns with smooth yarns. The result is a coarse, unfinished appearance. They may have a mixed colour effect as in tweeds and hopsacks or may be all one colour as in homespun or burlap.

CORDS/RIBS: These fabrics have a definite raised cord or ribbing on the surface, produced by alternating fine yarns with coarse yarns in a plain weave. Bedford cord has a heavy lengthwise rib; cotton broadcloth, poplin, faille and ottoman have crosswise ribs.

CREPE: A plain weave fabric with a crinkled or grainy surface formed by weaving various combinations of highly twisted yarns. The surface textures range from a fine, flat grain to a pebbly effect. Georgette and crepe de chine are sheer crepes; flat crepe is a medium-weight; satin crepe and satin-back crepe are heavy weights.

CRINKLED: Fabric with a permanently wrinkled or puckered effect may be done chemically or with heat setting. Seersucker, with crinkled stripes, is made by weaving some threads slackly, others tightly. The blistered surface of plisse and the crepe-like crinkle of cotton georgette are produced by chemically shrinking sections of the fabric. These

Knit fabrics are machine- or hand-made from all fibres and blends. Often in textures and patterns that simulate woven fabrics.

surfaces may also be embossed by using hot rollers, although this crinkle is not permanent. Woven crinkles are more lasting but may be flattened in ironing.

DOUBLE-FACED: Dual-personality fabrics with two right sides that can be used either side. Sides usually contrast in weave, texture or colour for fashion interest. Two layers of the same fabric may give double weight and extra stability and eliminate linings and facings. Double-faced fabrics are generally of three types:
(1) *Woven:* More than one set of warp or filling yarns is used to create a two-layered fabric with an interwoven design holding the two layers together. Design and colour are exactly reversed on each side. These fabrics cannot be separated for seaming (diag 1).

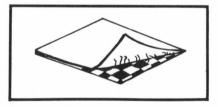

DIAGRAM 1

(2) *Bonded:* Two separate fabrics are first woven then joined back to back with an adhesive. This creates a lined effect or a reversible fabric, e.g., tricot backed jersey.

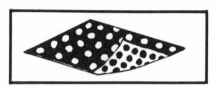

DIAGRAM 2

(3) *Connected with binding thread:* Double-faced fabrics are joined with a separate binding thread between the layers. This may easily be clipped so fabric will separate for concealed seams (diag 3).

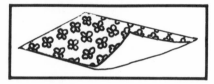

DIAGRAM 3

EYELET AND EMBROIDERY: Any fabric may have embroidery or decorative needlework designs applied by hand or machine. Eyelet has open-punched patterns with machine-embroidered buttonhole stitch on edges. Embroidery can be delicate or bold in design and colour.

FELT: Non-woven fabric that is made of matted fibres of wool, fur or mohair. It has a dull flat finish. Short fibres are matted by combination of heat, moisture and pressure.

JACQUARD: Fabrics with special weaving pattern that produces an elaborately woven design. Damask patterns stand out from the ground with a contrasting lustre. Brocade has heavy raised designs on a contrasting surface often using metallic threads.

KNITS: Fabric made by interlocking loops of one or more yarns. Main types are double knits, warp knits and tricot knits. Single knits such as jersey, drape softly but do not hold their shape as well as the double knits. Double knits look nearly the same on both sides, are firmer than jersey, yet still supple. Knit fabrics are made of all fibres and blends, often in textures and patterns. They have a natural stretch or elastic quality. Weights vary from gossamer to heavy coating weights. Novelty knits have tweed effects, lacy and mesh-like fabrics, loop knit and boucle surfaces. There are also jacquards, velours, ribbed ottomans and brocades.

LACE: This 'fabric' is an open fabric in which a delicate network consisting of a web of fine threads is formed into a design. Lace may be hand or machine-made from almost any fibre. When a motif is outlined with cord it is called re-embroidered lace.
Alencon and Chantilly: Light, delicate laces; usually a floral design on a fine net background.
Guipure: Coarser, stronger lace with geometric designs or floral motifs; usually cotton without mesh background.

LAMINATED: Term usually applied to fabric that is joined to a backing of synthetic foam; provides insulation and warmth with little weight or bulk, foam keeps garment shape and wrinkle free.

LUSTRE: Surface sheen on some fabrics increases light reflection on surface threads. A process of mercerisation of fabric or yarns such as chintz, polished cotton or sateen. The satin weave may produce this sheen, as in satin, sateen, Peau de Soie and taffeta where warp threads predominate over weft.

NAPPED: Fibrous surface is given to fabric. Some of the hairy or downy fibres are brought to the surface and then are either brushed for a soft effect or pressed flat to give a sheen. Napped fabrics such as wool broadcloth, fur fabrics, doeskin and suede cloth reflect light differently when slanting up than when slanting down so all pieces of a garment must be cut with the nap running in the same direction.

Plaids have a pattern of coloured stripes or bars crossing each other at right angles, printed or woven in any fabric.

Vinyl fabric is popular for rainwear because it is permanently waterproof.

Vinyl fabric is popular for rainwear because it is permanently waterproof.

SLUBBED: Fabrics having a roughness or unevenness in their weaves. The yarns have natural thick-and-thin areas (slubs) such as in silk doupion. honan and tussah. The 'slubs' may occur at random or regular intervals. Linen has a slightly slubbed effect due to occasional thicker places in the yarn. Rayon fabrics are often made with nobbles and slubs to give the effect of a natural unevenness. 'Linen-look' or 'silk-look' fabrics may not actually have any natural fibre in them.

PILE: Fabrics are woven with an extra set of looped yarns. The threads forming the pile are woven over cutting wires. When withdrawn they cut the loops to form tufts on velvet, velour and velveteen. Corduroy has fine-to-wide wales. 'Deep-pile' fabrics are especially thick, usually of man-made fibres and often imitate animal fur. Terry-cloth is a pile fabric with uncut loops.

PIQUE: Medium to heavyweight corded cotton cloth woven with lengthwise or crosswise ribs, or both. Pin-wale pique has very fine wales running lengthwise; wide-wale is similar, but wales are wider. Patterned piques: waffle pique has a woven honey-comb check; birdseye is a closely spaced, diamond-shaped design. Sculptured cottons with novelty patterns are sometimes classified as piques.

PLAIDS: Pattern of coloured stripes or bars crossing each other at right angles, printed or woven in any fabric.
Balanced plaid (or even): The plaid design is exactly the same on both lengthwise and cross-wise directions. They are the easiest plaids for sewing.
Uneven plaid: One in which the design is not the same in both lengthwise and crosswise directions. They are the most difficult plaids to use.

PRINTS: A general term given to any fabric that has a printed pattern or design applied after fabric is woven.

QUILTED: Two layers of fabric stitched together with padding between. Stitching may be done by hand or machine. Very often a pattern such as diamond-shaped, scroll or circle is used.

SHEER: Thin fabric with a transparent quality, generally a plain weave made from any fibre. Sheer fabrics may be soft and fluid or crisp.
Soft sheers: Have very little body, such as chiffon.
Semi-soft sheers: A heavier type of sheer, such as voile, lawn, dotted Swiss batiste, muslin.
Crisp sheers: Easiest to handle because they have a crisp durable finish, such as organdie, organza.

STRETCH: Specially constructed yarns woven in fabric to allow it to give with body movement then bounce back into shape. Stretch qualities add comfort, lengthwise stretch for slacks and ski pants, crosswise stretch for blouses and jackets.

TWEED: Fabric of rough, unfinished appearance and texture with a mixed colour effect, but may be plain colours, checks and plaids. Usually made of wool, but cotton, silk and synthetic tweeds are available.

TWILLS: There are several types of twill weaves. The basic twill runs up from left to right in a diagonal line. Variations include the herringbone formed by reversing direction of the twill at set intervals. Diagonal weaves are seen in rugged cotton denim, suit weights for tailoring such as gabardine, and lightweight surah.

VINYL: Fashion 'fabric' in clear film, printed or plain, is popular for rainwear and other garments because it is permanently waterproof. Vinyl films may be clear or fused to a knit or woven backing. Patent vinyl is shiny and slick. Vinyl with woven or knitted back may be embossed to simulate reptile skins and leather.

VINYL-COATED FABRICS: A base fabric, such as a printed or solid plain-weave cotton is coated with a thin layer of vinyl. Vinyl-coating is less expensive, light in weight but not permanently waterproof.

Finishes

TREATMENT applied to a fabric to add to its comfort and ease of care or to enhance its appearance or feel is called finish. Finishes of some kind are applied to most fabrics; 'special' finishes add qualities the fibre may lack and makes them perform more effectively. The three basic finishes are termed:
Non-durable: Lasts only until the first washing or dry cleaning.
Durable: Lasts through several washings or cleanings.
Permanent: Effective for life of fabric and garment.
Here are the 'special' finish terms most generally used on fabrics.

COLOURFAST: This term means that colours do not noticeably change for the life of the fabric. Colours should not rub off and should resist fading from laundering, dry cleaning, sunlight, perspiration, or ironing.

A shirt dress is a useful item for anyone's wardrobe. Select the right fabric to achieve figure
flattery with this style.

CREASE RESISTANT/WRINKLE RESISTANT: Finish applied to cotton, linen and rayon to resist creases and help the fabric to shed wrinkles.

DRIP-DRY: Minimum-care finish for fabrics which after washing, and without wringing, are hung on a hanger to 'drip dry'. Garments after laundering should have a minimum of wrinkles and cottons should require little or no ironing.

DURABLE-PRESS: The most advanced in wash-and-wear finishes; a combination of a chemical finish plus heat-setting to give fabric permanent press finish, it keeps creases in and wrinkles out through repeated washings. In ready-to-wear fashions it enables the fabric to be permanently pleated or creased when heat-setting is applied *after* the garment is made. This finish makes it nearly impossible to alter a garment, since pleat marks remain.

Durable-Press or Permanent Press finish is available on piecegoods, 100 percent cotton and cotton/polyester blends. They need modified sewing techniques to prevent puckering along seam lines and zip closures.

STAIN AND SPOT RESISTANT: This finish has previously been used on home furnishing fabrics but is now often applied to fashion fabrics to resist stains caused by water and oily substances; stains will not penetrate the fibres and may be wiped off.

SHRINKAGE CONTROL: Treatments to fabric to remove most of its tendency to shrink. 'Residual shrinkage' is the percentage of shrinkage left in the fabric after application of a shrinking process. *Pre-shrunk:* Will not shrink more than 3 percent. *Sanforized®:* Special finish applied to cotton or linen, guarantees less than 1 percent shrinkage in length or width.

WASHABLE: Term describing fabrics which will not noticeably fade or shrink when they are washed. Directions are usually given for hand or machine washing and correct water temperature. Special processes on some all-wool fabrics are now making them completely machine washable.

WASH-AND-WEAR: Various finishes that are applied to fabrics which require little or no ironing after laundering come under this heading. With crease resistant finishes, the amount of pressing necessary varies from 'no-iron' to 'touch-up' depending on fibre content, durability of finish, and the appropriate laundering method. 'Automatic wash-and-wear' means the fabric can be washed and dried in an automatic washer and dryer.

WATERPROOF: This finish creates a smooth unbroken fabric surface so that no moisture or air can penetrate it; usually it is a coating of rubber, resin or plastic, such as vinyl, to close spaces between yarns. These fabrics do not 'breathe' and can be uncomfortable to wear.

WATER-REPELLENT/RESISTANT: Finish applied to fabrics to make them resist penetration by water but it does not close the space between yarns. Fabric can 'breathe' and is more comfortable to wear. Spray-on finish is available in cans.

How to Sew Fashion Fabrics

CHOOSE your fabrics carefully, making sure they suit both your pattern and your figure. A fabric can make you appear larger or smaller, taller or shorter, older or younger.

There is a world of new fabrics that add to the pleasure of creative sewing. Deep-pile, vinyls, bonded and stretch fabrics take their place beside the classic favourites of knits, plaids and stripes, lace, sheer, printed and pile fabrics. There are leathers and suedes, real and imitation. They all add up to the wonderful world of fashion fabrics.

Each fabric needs some special handling, so here are the extra pointers you need to sew them successfully:

1. Always check the back of the pattern envelope for fabric and yardage suggestions. You will find a wealth of information there on suitability of fabric to the design. You will find 'with nap' yardages given for designs suitable for napped fabrics. 'Nap' as used in patterns, means any one-way fabric or fabric with a definite up-and-down pattern or design.

2. Read fabric labels carefully and follow instructions for preparation, cutting, sewing, pressing or care.

3. If your fabric has special texture interest or design, choose a simple pattern style (avoiding intricate seams, and other detail), the fabric itself is all-important.

If however, your fabric is one of the classic types, this is your chance to use a more detailed or tailored pattern, with lots of seaming.

4. Always make any necessary alterations on the pattern. This will avoid changes after the garment is cut and stitched.

5. Use fine pins, sharp shears and needles.

6. Along the cutting edge of some patterns are printed ◆ which are called notches. They indicate where parts of the garment are to be matched and joined as the garment is constructed.

Cut notches outwards (never in); for double or triple notches, cut across top of notches on solid line.

7. Some patterns are specifically designed to include underlining, or lining (some laces and sheers, for example). In other cases, an underlining or lining is left to your discretion.

If an underlining or lining is needed, cut garment and lining from the same pattern. For underlining, baste fabric and underlining pieces together, then sew as one. Linings are made separately and joined at the major seams, such as the waistline.

8. Before stitching, always test the sewing machine setting on a folded scrap of fabric. Check to be sure the needle size, type of thread and stitch length are suitable for the fabric to be sewn. Make any adjustments to stitch length, and tension.

9. Layer bulky seams that will be enclosed, such as inside a collar, cuff or facing. This means that the seams are trimmed away with one seam allowance narrower than the other. The uppermost seam allowance should be the widest to prevent a bulky ridge from showing after pressing.

10. Press as you sew, since proper pressing is one of the things that helps make a garment look professionally made.

Stretch Fabrics

STRETCH in a fabric means it gives with body movement, adds comfort, shape retention, wrinkle resistance and longer wear. Specially constructed yarns woven into fabric make it stretch when pulled—then bounce back into shape.

There are three types of stretch fabrics:

Filling (horizontal) *stretch:* Crosswise from selvage to selvage. Used for blouses, shirts, dresses, jackets and skirts.

Warp (up and down or vertical) *stretch:* Lengthwise or parallel to selvages. Best for pants.

Two-way stretch: In both directions. Up to now, used mostly in swimsuits and foundation garments.

Stretch is being applied to an ever-widening range of fabrics, lightweight batistes, broadcloth,

Denim is a strong fabric that launders well and is popular for work and play clothes.

pique and seersucker; firmly woven denims, gabardines, wool flannels, poplins, twills, corduroys and tweeds. Far greater comfort and freedom of movement in all types of fashion has come with the introduction of stretch fabrics.

Purchasing fabric:
• Test the direction of the stretch to be sure it is that needed for the garment. Pants may be made from a filling stretch fabric if it is wide enough to lay pattern along crosswise grain. In this way, stretch will still run from waist to ankle.

Patterns:
• Use patterns for stretch fabrics in your usual size. Make pattern alterations in the usual way. Pants should have a stirrup under the foot.

Handling:
• If not labelled 'pre-shrunk', shrink fabric by steam pressing. Use heat setting suitable to fibre content. Press lightly and lift iron to avoid stretching fabric. Before cutting, lay the fabric smooth and flat for about 24 hours.

Layout:
• Place pattern on the fabric so that stretch runs in the required direction: *across the shoulders* for blouses, shirts, dresses and jackets; *from waist to ankle* in pants, slacks or shorts; *from side to side* in skirts. Lay waistband in non-stretch direction.

Cutting:
• Avoid stretching the fabric as you work. Roll or fold excess so it is all on table and do not let fabric hang over edges of cutting table. Place pins perpendicular to stretch direction.

Sewing machine:
• Pressure: Medium to light.
• Stitch length: Short—14-15 stitches per inch.
• Needle: Fine to medium—size 11 to 14.
• Thread: Textured nylon or nylon threads have more 'give' with stretch seams than mercerised. With a straight stitch and nylon thread maintain stretch in the seams by stretching fabric slightly as you stitch. Reinforce the seam with a second row of stitching sewn close to first, a small zigzag stitch allows greater stretch in seams. Experiment first with test threads to be sure stitching won't break when seam is pulled.

Sewing tips:
• Interfacing: May be used as usual on garment where stretch is not important.
• Lining: If needed, use only a stretch lining or bias-cot tricot. Lining must stretch in same direction as outer fabric. Do not sew lining into side seams —join to garment at neck and waistline seams.

• Slide fastener: Hand-baste in position. Ease fabric, do not stretch. Sew fastener in by hand or machine. Keep opposite seam firm for length of fastener so both sides will hang in same way.
• Buttonholes: Make them perpendicular to stretch direction. Strengthen with a small patch of iron-on or firmly woven interfacing.
• Hems: Zigzag stitch ¼in from edge or use bias seam binding. On heavier fabrics, stitch ¼in from edge or overcast. Loosely slipstitch hem in place.

Pressing:
• Use steam or setting suitable to fibre content. Lift iron to avoid stretch or pull on fabric.

Bonded Fabrics

BONDED fabrics have a lining permanently fused to the woven or knitted outer fabric. The added body creates a stable fabric structure and wrinkle resistance; fabrics will not stretch or fray, need no interfacing or interlining and little pressing. The smooth, silky backing adds new comfort and a lining to fabrics such as wool flannel, jersey and lace.

Purchasing fabric:
• Check for a straight grain. These fabrics cannot be easily straightened if bonded off grain.

Patterns:
• Simple patterns are best. Remember some bonded fabrics are soft, some stiff, some fine, some bulky.

Handling:
• The fabrics are pre-shrunk, stable and firm. Fabrics cannot be straightened, cut garment following lengthwise grain or rib: crosswise grain may not be straight but appearance or wear of garment will not be affected.

Cutting and marking:
• Place pattern on right side of fabric where grain line shows.
• Cut single thickness for best results. For pieces cut on fold: cut first half, flip pattern over on fold line; cut other half.
• If possible, cut garment and facing in one to eliminate seam.
• Mark with tailor tacks.

Sewing machine:
• Tension and pressure: Medium to light.
• Stitch length: Medium to long.
• Needle: Fine to medium—size 11 to 14.

Even plaids in which the designs are balanced in both the lengthwise and crosswise direction are the easiest plaids to work with.

Printed fabrics need special handling so you should always choose a pattern which is specifically designed for the fabric.

• Thread: Use any suitable for outer fabric content. Modern sewing machines usually have a special stitch setting that sews stretch into the seams of knitted fabrics.

Sewing tips:
• Hand-baste and fit to avoid stitch marks.
• No seam finish is needed if fabric does not ravel.
• Darts: Press darts flat as shown (diag 1).

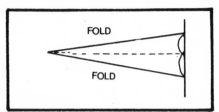

DIAGRAM I

• Seam finishes: Some fabrics are springy, press open and topstitch close to seam line. Or, trim one edge close to seam line, press and stitch other edge over it (diag 2)—this prevents seam allowance from rolling.

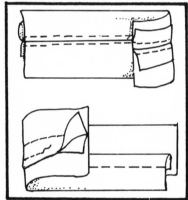

DIAGRAM 2

• Facings: On heavy fabrics, reduce bulk by using a lining fabric for facings. Or substitute a braid-trimmed edge.
• Buttonholes: Reinforce with strips of lightweight fabric.
• Hems: Hem tricot-bonded garments through lining only.

Pressing:
• Use steam or dry iron at heat setting suitable for outer fabric. Test before pressing garment. Use dry or damp press cloth to protect tricot lining.

Knits

KNITTED fabrics are made in a variety of fibres— natural and synthetic—and lend comfort and a fluid elegance to every fashion. Some are sold in tubular form; others are sold flat.

Single Knits drape softly. Double Knits are not difficult to handle. They are in double stitch and firmer, yet still flexible; they tailor beautifully and usually do not need underlining.

Purchasing fabric:
• The lengthwise rib is the 'straight-of-grain'. Check to be sure rib is not severely twisted out of line. It is better not to buy fabric with a prominent weave, if it is more than ½in off grain, it cannot be straightened.
• Weight can be your guide in choosing knit jersey: fine for blouses; medium weights for dresses; heavy weights for suits and coats.
• Lining slim skirts and completely underlining the loose knits helps them retain their shape.

Patterns:
• The pattern envelope will guide you with knit fabric suggestions.
• 'Designed for Knit Fabrics Only' styles are for stretchable, unbonded knits. These patterns have little or no ease and often darts may have been omitted. For a good-looking garment, use a knit with lots of stretch, or 'give', for these styles. At times patterns will include one or two views for stretchable knits only, while other views will be for woven fabrics and knits that are firm and stable or bonded.
• 'Ideal for Knits' styles have the usual amount of ease and fit equally well in woven fabrics. Use a knit that's firm and stable, or one that's bonded, for these styles.

Preparation:
• All knit fabrics, except tricot backed jersey should be pre-shrunk before cutting.
• If using a tubular knit, cut along one rib close to the fold line to open it.
• Check 'grain' of fabric; pull gently on bias to straighten.
• Press out folds of tubular knit, if folds will not press out completely. Place pattern on fabric so creases will not be prominent on finished garment.

Cutting out:
• Look closely at right side of knitted fabric before pinning pattern pieces to it. Align lengthwise pattern marking with lengthwise rib.
• Lay fabric flat on sewing table, avoid stretching while pinning and cutting. Remember knits stretch more in width than in length.
• Since some patterns include views for both stretchable and stable knits, check to make sure you use the correct layout and pattern pieces. Some tricots, jerseys and stretch terries curl up at the edges, making layout tedious. In these cases

it's easiest to lay out the pattern on the wrong side of the fabric and to place pins at right angles to the seam lines.

Sewing machine:
- Tension: Medium to light.
- Stitch length: 12-15 per inch, or a small zigzag.
- Needle: For lightweight knits—size 11 (fine); Double and heavier knits—medium size 14.
- Thread: Terylene, nylon, or mercerised cotton, depending on fibrous content of knit.

Sewing tips:
- In lightweight knits: Stay-stitch shoulders and neckline, and reinforce shoulder and waistline with pre-shrunk woven seam tape to prevent stretching.
- Interfacing: Use on faced edges and under buttonholes to reinforce. Also on waistbands.
- On bulky knits, cut facing of lining fabric.
- Lining: Cut lining pieces same as garment. Wrong sides together, stitch knit to lining pieces ½in from edge and sew as one fabric. For skirt and one-piece dress, make lining separately. Join to bodice at neckline and armhole; and at waistline. At hem, finish lining separately, about 1in shorter than dress. Knits do not ravel so special seam finishes are not needed.
- Make tailor's hem (let knit garments hang a day before hemming): Pink, machine edge—stitch raw edge of hem; catch loosely to garment (diag 3).

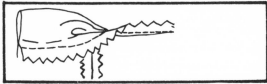

DIAGRAM 3

To hold an A-line shape at the hem of a dress or skirt, a layer of lightweight woven interfacing cut on the bias should be used to back the hem. Cut bias strips 1in wider than, and the length of, the hem; pin to wrong side of the hem, the lower edge ½in below hem fold. Baste to garment, then follow the steps for a catch-stitched hem. Remove basting stitches.

To make a catch-stitched hem, finish the raw edge with a row of machine stitches, either straight (about 10 stitches to the inch) or zigzag. No hem tape, other than a stretch lace type for purely decorative purposes, is required. Baste hem in place ¼in from the raw edge. Fold hem back ¼in on the wrong side and catch-stitch loosely to garment (diag 4). Press hem lightly.

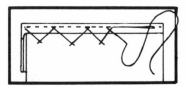

DIAGRAM 4

- Set-in sleeves: With the side seams open and the garment flat, pin sleeve to garment at underarm, notches, shoulder seam, and a few strategic places here and there in between to distribute the ease (diag 5). No basting is necessary. Sew sleeve to the garment, stretching as you sew. Sew the side and sleeve seams in one continuous stitching line. Diag 6 shows how the garment will look from the back when this is done.
- Slide fasteners: Setting the slide fastener in the fabric by hand works best on stretchable knits. Here is a quick way to position the fastener. Use transparent adhesive or masking tape to hold the

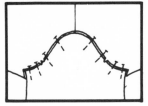 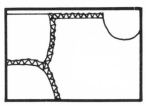

DIAGRAM 5   DIAGRAM 6

fastener and seam allowances in position (diag 7). Hand pick the fastener. Use silk buttonhole twist or embroidery thread and take tiny backstitches. Work from bottom of fastener to neckline (diag 8).

DIAGRAM 7   DIAGRAM 8

- Knit slacks: To prevent baggy knees in slacks made from stretchy knits, borrow this idea from the makers of expensive imported knit slacks. As shown in finished form in diag 9, sew pieces of lightweight, non-stretch fabric in the seams of each leg at the knee.

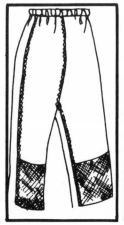 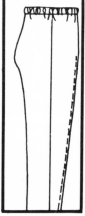

DIAGRAM 9   DIAGRAM 10

Knitted fabrics are in fashion for clothes that are practical, comfortable and good-looking.

Although slacks from polyester or wool knit will hold a heat-set crease, those from cotton knits resist neat creases. The stitched-down crease, shown in diag 10, is the solution. First fold the finished slacks so side seam and inner leg seam meet. Press crease on the front only, stopping about 6in from the waist. Baste crease. Stitch by machine, as close to the edge of the crease as possible. Remove basting stitches.

Pressing:
• Press with lengthwise rib. Lift and lower iron; do not stretch or pull fabric.

Nylon jersey

Cutting:
• Use fine pins, place in seam allowance.

Sewing machine:
• Tension: Loosen tension of upper and bobbin heads.
• Stitch length: Use about 12 stitches per inch.
• Needle: Sharp, fine—size 11. Change the needle when it becomes dull. Hold fabric taut in front and behind presser foot as you stitch to help prevent puckers.

Sewing tips:
• Pin-baste in seam lines to prevent pin marks from showing. Stitch at a slow, even speed to prevent puckering.
• Hems: Stitch or zigzag edge. Hand-sew hem loosely to prevent puckering.

• Wide hems and double hems add body. Allow 3in hem on straight skirt, 2in on full skirts. If not allowed for on your pattern, be sure to purchase enough fabric to allow for a deep hem.

Patterns:
• Patterns designed for sheers are best, as they include all instructions for that final finish.
• Tucks are easier to make on the crisp sheers.
• Select a pattern with as few seams as possible.

Handling:
• Sheers have a tightly woven selvage which may cause the fabric to 'buckle'. If so, clip through the entire depth of the selvage every few inches.

Cutting and marking:
• Soft sheers may shift, so pin to tissue paper to prevent the fabric from shifting. Cut with very sharp shears. Remove the paper, then mark construction details.
• When possible, cut full gathered skirts on the crosswise grain to eliminate some seams.
• Sleeves are generally cut from a single layer of fabric.
• Using sheer alone, eliminate facing at neckline, sleeves or armholes and use a French binding of self material.
    Take a ¾in bias strip of the fabric, fold it in half lengthwise, and lightly press. Taking ⅛in seam allowance on the cut edges, baste the double bias to right side of neckline ¼in lower than the finished neckline is to be. Slightly stretch bias as you baste. Machine stitch, turn bias to wrong side of dress and slip-stitch folded edge to stitchline (diag. 11).

Delicate Fabrics— Sheers and Laces

DIAGRAM 11

SHEER fabrics are always firm favourites for 'special' occasions. In both bouffant and slim styles, sheers impart a graceful feeling, an enchanting feminine look.
    There are three types of sheer fabrics:
Soft and fluid sheers—such as chiffon.
Semi-soft sheers—such as voile, lawn, dimity.
Crisp sheers—such as organdie. Crisp sheers are easiest to handle.

Purchasing fabric:
• Sheers can be lined or worn with a separate slip. (Sleeves and upper bodices can remain unlined.) Choose linings carefully to give depth, interest or opaqueness to sheer fabric.

On the full soft sheers a wide hem is often used. On circular skirts a narrow hem. Straight and A-line skirts have the normal 2¼in hem.

Sewing machine:
• Tension: Average to loose, depending on fabric and thread.
• Stitch length: About 14-16 stitches per inch.
• Needle: Very fine—size 9 to 10.
• Thread: Fine thread suitable to fabric, or mercerised cotton thread.

Sewing tips:
• Soft sheers: To prevent marring surface when sewing, stitch against strips of tissue paper, handling paper and fabric as one.

An unusual fabric combination of fake leather and fake fur makes a smart garment suitable for many occasions.

• Seams and seam finishes:

(1) Double stitched seam. Stitch a plain seam. Make a second row of stitching about ⅛in from the seam line, within the seam allowance. Trim seam close to this stitching.

(2) Make a narrow French seam. First, with wrong sides together, sew the seam ¼in outside the stitching line (within the seam allowance). Trim the seam allowance to ⅛in; press, turn to wrong side and stitch again ¼in from edge encasing the raw edges. Press to one side.

(3) The almost-invisible seam. (a) Right sides together, stitch ⅛in from seam line within the seam allowance. (b) Fold and press both layers of seam to one side along stitching line. Stitch again, close to folding edge. (c) Trim off seam allowance close to stitching. (d) Turn seam to wrong side; stitch close to edge (diag 12).

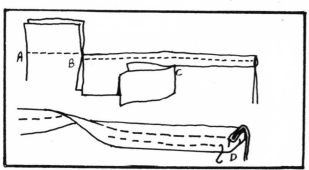

DIAGRAM 12

• Buttonholes: Machine buttonholes are usually best on sheers.

• Hems. Turn hem to inside; turn edge under ¼in and stitch. Slip-stitch hem in place.

• Double fold hems: Turn hem up desired depth; turn up again so raw edge is in fold.

• Narrow hem: Fold fabric to wrong side ⅛in outside marked hemline and press. Stitch as close to the edge as possible. Trim off excess fabric close to stitching. Turn the stitched edge to the wrong side again; press. Stitch again close to edge. For a circular skirt use a narrow, hand-rolled hem.

Lace

Lace lends its special charm to clothes. Laces vary from heavy cotton to delicate silk and nylon and wool. Despite its fragile look, lace often masks strength, wrinkle resistance and ease-of-care.

Purchasing fabric:

• Weight and type of lace, all-over pattern, a one-way or panel design are important considerations.

• Net makes the lace design stand out; an opaque underlining eliminates transparency. Sew lightweight laces to the underlinings for body and support. Make linings from fine silk for softly-draped lines, taffeta for crisp bouffant effects, organza for a semi-sheer look. Bonded laces

where lining is fused to lace are available.

• Not all laces need to be underlined. You can make a separate matching or contrasting slip.

• Jackets and coats can be lined in the usual way.

Patterns:

• The right pattern will show the lace to best advantage. Look for simple lines, and use a minimum number of seams and darts to keep lace motif intact.

Cutting and marking:

• Place pattern pieces carefully to show lace design at its best.

• If matching is needed, match at seams and front openings.

• Cut underlining pieces from the same pattern as the garment. For more formal designs, leave sleeves and upper part of bodice unlined, or use chiffon or net for underlining upper bodice.

• Facings: In heavy laces, cut from lining fabric. For unlined or sheer garments, cut from matching net. An elegant finish is achieved by edging with binding cut from chiffon or satin.

• For lined garments, mark construction details on the wrong side of the lining pieces only. For unlined laces, use tailor tacks.

Sewing machine:

• Tension: Slightly loose.

• Pressure: Adjust to fabric.

• Stitch length: Medium to long—15 stitches per inch.

• Needle: Fine—size 11.

• Thread: Mercerised, nylon or silk, depending on fabric.

Sewing tips:

• Construction linings: With right side of lining and wrong side of lace together, sew along all edges except hem, and treat as one fabric when putting garment together. All seams will be hidden.

• Darts: Stitch lace-and-lining fabric together down the centre line of the dart to hold in place.

• In unlined heavier laces darts are easier to stitch if slashed open first to within ⅝in of point. Stitch; press edges open, trim back to ¼in.

• Hold lined heavy laces together with a line of machine stitching through *outline* of dart. Stitch dart and finish.

• Seams: Stitch fine laces over tissue paper.

• Seam finishes: For laces with opaque linings, use a plain seam; pink, stitch or overcast edges. For unlined laces stitch on seam line then stitch, or zigzag, ¼in from seam line within seam allowance. Trim close to stitching and press to one side.

• Armhole seams: Make second row of stitching ¼in from seam line in seam allowance. Trim, press.

• For gathered or soft-pleated skirts: Stitch side seams of lace and lining pieces *separately*. Then

place right side of lining to wrong side of lace. Join together along upper edges and along seam lines of left side opening. Gather or pleat as if one fabric. Hem lining and lace separately.
• Facings: Underlined garments, hand-sew facing edges to lining only. Finish edges of net facings with row of straight or zigzag stitching.
• Slide fasteners: Stitch lace-and-lining fabric together along seam lines at fastener closing. Insert fastener using hand stitches for a more invisible closure.
• Buttonholes: Machine buttonholes are best. Some sewing machines have a special cam for making buttonholes on lace.
• Hems: With underlined garments trim underlining so edge comes to crease of hem and finish edge with seam tape. Catch hem to underlining.
• In unlined garments, make hem by:
(1) Running a line of machine stitching ¼in from trimmed raw edge of lace. Hand-stitch hem in place. (2) Finishing edge with zigzag stitch then hand-stitch in place. (3) Or, turn edge up ⅝in and stitch ¼in horsehair braid through hem allowance and skirt. Trim lace close to braid.

Pressing:
• Set iron for fibre content of fabric. Press from wrong side with lace over dowel to prevent flattening.

Leathers, Suedes and Vinyls

ANIMAL skins are fashionable. They come in smooth, supple leather and napped suede. These skins make fashion garments of classic and lasting beauty.

Purchasing skins:
• Leather and suede are bought by the skin. Choose skins uniform in weight and colour.
• Buy your pattern first and lay out pattern pieces to determine how many skins you will need.
• Interfacings are important for holding shape.

Patterns:
• Patterns should be simple with straight lines, few seams, darts and details.

Cutting:
• Avoid waste in cutting. Trim pattern seams to ⅜in to reduce bulk.
• Eliminate seams if possible—such as straight centre back seam. A complete paper pattern for front and back should be cut and used.

• Lay skins flat. Place the complete pattern on a single layer of skin to plan your cutting out.
• If skin is not wide enough to make a complete front or back, cut two separate pieces and seam in the centre. Add seam allowance when cutting.
• Smooth leather—place pattern pieces all lengthwise or crosswise on right side of skins. Suede—cut with tops of all pieces pointing to neck of the skin—so that 'nap' will lie in the same direction.
• Pin marks will show, so hold pattern pieces in place with weights or tape pattern to skins.
• Mark darts, sewing details with chalk on wrong side.
• Extend front interfacing to armhole for strength.
• Cut facings from skins or lining fabric. Or, line to edge with taffeta to reduce bulk.

Sewing machine:
• Tension: Balanced, slightly loose.
• Pressure: Light; adjust to weight of skins.
• Stitch length: Long—7 to 10 stitches per inch.
• Needle: Use a special wedge-shaped machine needle for stitching leather.
• Thread: Heavy-duty mercerised or synthetic.

Sewing tips:
• Needle marks will show. Stitch with care to avoid ripping. Do not stretch as you stitch.
• Darts: Stitch, slash, flatten, glue in place.
• Seams: Avoid pins. Use paper clips to hold layers together. Do not backstitch; tie thread ends.
• Stitch seams. Press seams open and flatten with a mallet. Then glue seams flat. Spread a thin line of fabric glue or rubber cement over stitches on both sides of seam line; press seam open, using brown paper 'press cloth'. On curved seams, cut out small 'Vs' before finishing so that seam will be flat.
• Attach lining to facing. (1) Bind facing with bias tape and hand stitch lining to binding. (2) Or, glue lining under edge of facing.
• Buttonholes: Always test first on scrap of leather. (1) Use bound buttonholes on soft leather. (2) Machine buttonholes—stitch rectangle close to slash marking. Stitch again just outside this first row—slash.
• Hems: Make one or two inches wide. Turn up then glue and hammer lightly in place.

Pressing:
• Do not use steam. Press with warm dry iron over a dry press cloth or brown paper.

Vinyls
The look of beautifully tanned leathers has been faked so expertly in ways that only an expert tanner can tell the difference. They are being used for dresses, suits, pants, capes, jackets and a whole range of accessories.

Analyse a striped fabric before you buy it. Always keep the dress pattern in mind and try to visualise whether the stripes will have the effect on your figure that you desire.

Purchasing fabric:
There are three basic types of leather-like fabrics: *Vinyl surface* with a cotton backing has smooth or antiqued finishes. They are light in weight, often machine washable.

Cotton canvas, with a resin or plastic-coated outer surface, is washable and can be dry cleaned. It may be ironed lightly and carefully on the wrong side.

Nylon knit has an embossed surface to look like soft, sleek kid. This can be washed and pressed very lightly.

Patterns:
• When you begin working with these fake leathers, choose a simple pattern. Raglan or kimono sleeves are the easiest.

Cutting and marking:
• Interlinings are recommended in buttonhole and neckline area.
• Cut single thicknesses only.
• Linings are used in jackets and coats for comfort.
• Keep the fabric rolled until ready for use to prevent creasing.
• Pin the fabric in seam allowances only, as pin marks show.

Sewing tips:
• A medium tension and light pressure will do for the machine.
As fabrics respond differently to machines, test first before doing the seams.
• Use a tailor's hem or rubber cement to fix the the hemline.

Mohair and Diagonal Fabrics

SOFTLY SPUN mohair is strong and lustrous. Classic sportswear and separates, dresses, jackets and coats look great in this fabric.

Mohair may be woven or knit, looped or brushed and is often combined with other fibres in fabrics that are bulky but lightweight.

Purchasing fabric:
• Buy yardage given for fabrics 'with nap'—refer to back of pattern envelope.
• Knit mohair: Dry clean only, do not steam press or sponge in preparing fabric for cutting, during making up or in care of garment.
• Underline with firm backing or, for a soft effect, use lightweight fabric such as thin silk.

Patterns:
• Simply styled lines complement the bulky fabric. Avoid pleats. Select pattern with minimum of seams.

Cutting:
• Refold knit mohair to avoid the original pressed-in side creases used in manufacturing.
• Use nap layout—with loops or nap running *down*.
• Do not stretch fabric as you cut.
• Mark with tailor tacks.

Sewing machine:
• Tension: Loosen tension upper and bobbin threads.
• Stitch length: Average—12 stitches per inch.
• Needle: Medium—size 14.
• Thread: Mercerised.

Sewing tips:
• Stitch slowly and carefully to avoid catching loops on presser foot. Stitch with tissue paper placed between both sides of fabric and machine.
• Seams: Overcast, bind or zigzag seam edges.
• Bound buttonholes: To hold shape, back with a matching firm fabric. For corded buttonholes, interface strips that cover cord with same backing.

Pressing:
• Use a dry iron and very little heat. *Never* steam press; steam will shrink the fabric and flatten the texture of the surface.

Diagonal fabrics
Diagonal fabrics have a prominent twill weave. Woven diagonal lines of the same or contrasting colour appear on fabric surface. They require no special sewing tips, but the right pattern and proper cut are all-important. Diagonals cannot be matched when a bias seam is used.

Purchasing fabric:
• Remember that many twill weaves—such as gabardine, silk surah and denim—are so closely woven that the diagonal line is not prominent. But some of these fabrics may show a colour difference between pieces joined on the bias.

Patterns:
• Check back of pattern envelope—some designs are marked 'not suitable' for diagonal fabrics.
• Simple styles, slim skirts, few seams, set-in sleeves and straight underarm darts are best.
• When using prominent diagonals avoid bias seams, long bias darts, wide A-line or gored skirts, long kimono sleeves and deep V-necklines.

Cutting:
• If pattern is carefully selected you can follow the regular cutting layout. Experiment with

placing collars, waistbands, pockets and other trimming details to see which way you want the diagonal lines to run.

• For a definite diagonal pattern, cut garment so diagonal lines run from upper left side towards lower right in garment front, and from upper right to lower left in garment back. The diagonal continues around figure in same direction.

• Chevron: You can form chevrons if the fabric is identical on both sides. Open fabric to its full width. Measure pattern pieces being used for chevrons to determine length. Cut this length twice. Place the right side of one piece against the wrong side of the other. Place your pattern pieces on the double layer following pattern layout.

Nap and Pile Fabrics

BOTH nap and pile add a special look to a fabric, giving it a feeling of warmth and luxury.

Napped fabrics—such as wool broadcloth and fleecy fabrics—have had fibres raised from the body of the cloth. These are brushed for soft effect or pressed flat to give a sheen.

Pile fabrics are woven with an extra set of looped yarns; these are clipped to form the special textures of fabrics such as corduroy, velveteen and velvet.

Purchasing fabric:
• Buy the yardage given on your pattern envelope for fabrics 'with nap'. The pattern will include a layout for napped, pile or any fabric which must be cut with the tops of all pieces pointing in the same direction.

Patterns:
• Choose a simple design that will emphasise the fabric. Look for minimum of seams, darts, tucks.

Cutting and marking:
• Pile reflects light differently when it slants up than when it slants down. Run your hand along the grain. The nap running *down* has a smoother feeling and lighter, shinier look. Nap or pile running *up* has a rougher touch, richer colour.

• In general, cut napped fabrics (such as wool broadcloth) with nap running *down*. Corduroy cut this way wears longer.

• For richer colour cut most *pile* weaves such as velvet and velveteen, with nap running *up*.

• Important: The nap on all pieces must run in the same direction. Place pattern pieces on fabric with tops all pointing the same way.

• Cut velvet, velveteen and corduroy with *right* sides on outside to prevent the pile from matting together. The corduroy rib also is easier to follow.

• To prevent velvet from slipping, pin the fabric edges together before placing the pattern. On delicate fabrics pin in seam allowances only.

• Baste with silk thread to prevent marks when it is removed.

Sewing machine:
• Tension and pressure: Light.
• Stitch length: About 10 stitches per inch.
• Needle: Fine.
• Thread: Mercerised for corduroy, velveteen; silk or mercerised for woollens, velvets.

Sewing tips:
• Seams: Use silk thread to baste before machine stitching to prevent slippage and puckered seams. Always sew in the direction of nap or pile.

• Seam finishes: Turned edges leave press-marks on right side. Pink or overcast seams or zigzag raw edges. Bind seam edges that ravel in seam tape.

• Gathering: Hand-gather with ¼in stitches and ¼in spaces. To keep threads from breaking, use silk, nylon or heavy-duty thread on corduroy.

• Facings: Use lightweight fabrics such as organza or taffeta for velvets and velveteens, and light-weight cotton for washable garments.

• Hem and facing finishes: Pink and stitch or zigzag raw edge or stitch bias, seam binding to edge; loosely catch hem to garment as for tailor's hem.

Pressing
• To open seams in velvet, stand iron on end and place a damp cloth over it. Hold the wrong side of the velvet by the seams and run along the covered iron (diag 13).

Fake furs
Cleverly faked—you would take them for real, the latest designs in these deep-pile fabrics bring the luxury look of fur into every woman's wardrobe. This year's fashion 'animal kingdom' fabrics include leopard, pony, zebra, lamb and tiger. The pile is usually synthetic with either a knitted or woven backing of cotton, acrylic or other fibre.

Purchasing fabric:
• Follow yardage charts and layouts for fabrics 'with nap'.

• Read labels: Some of these pile fabrics may be washed—others must be dry cleaned.

DIAGRAM 13

Patterns:
• Simple designs (with few seams in coats, jackets), accessories and a fashion favourite—sleeveless pop-overs. Avoid collars, set-in sleeves or buttonholes and inset pockets.

Cutting:
• When using double width fabric cut pattern in one piece to eliminate straight centre back seams. If possible, cut straight facings in one with garment or from lighter weight matching fabric. If suitable, bind edges with braid.
• Place pattern on wrong side with tops of all pattern pieces in same direction. Cut so pile runs *down*. With very deep pile, cut in single layers. Pile may be easier to handle if you cut with a razor blade from the wrong side, as for fur.

Sewing machine:
• Tension: Loose.
• Pressure: Light.
• Stitch length: 8-10 stitches per inch.
• Needle: Medium size.
• Thread: Mercerised cotton thread.

Sewing tips:
• It helps to hand-baste fabric to prevent 'creeping' and puckering while machine stitching.
• Seams: Stitch in direction of pile wherever possible. Reinforce points of strain with seam tape. Use pin to lift pile caught in stitched seam to right side.
• Where facings do not show use taffeta facings to eliminate bulk of deep pile fabrics.
• Darts: To finish, cut open and press flat, using tip of iron only.
• On deep pile use bias hem facing and catch-stitch hem to backing. For other piles finish raw edge with stretch lace seam binding. Overcast catching seam binding to backing.

Pressing:
• Prevent flattening of pile by placing it pile side down on velvet board, with press cloth over backing. Steam lightly, holding iron above fabric. If two pile sides (such as front facing) must be pressed, turn one end of a terry towel up over facing.

How to press napped fabrics
• For fabrics with a brushed nap, press in the direction in which the nap runs. Use a light pressure and a slightly damp press cloth with a dry iron. After pressing, brush lightly with the nap.
• For fabrics with unbrushed nap place a piece of wool fabric over the ironing board. Place right side of the garment against the wool. Press on the wrong side. While the fabric is still steaming, brush with the grain of the fabric.

How to press pile fabrics
• The best results are obtained by using a velvet pressing board or, as it is often called, a needle board. This is a heavy backing canvas covered with wire bristles called 'needles'. Place the pile side against the needles and press lightly, the needles prevent the pile being crushed (diag 14).

DIAGRAM 14

If the garment has a facing of pile fabric, place in between two velvet pressing boards or turn one end of the board over the facing. Use a steam iron or damp cloth with dry iron over the top board.

As an alternative to a velvet board, stand a dry iron on its heel; place a damp press cloth over the wrong side of the fabric and pass the garment back and forth over the iron so the steam penetrates the pile.

Another substitute is to lay the fabric pile side down over a heavy terry towel (or a pad covered with a towel) and press lightly with a steam iron or a damp cloth.

47

Glamour Fabrics

THERE is nothing more feminine or more elegant to wear for summer's special occasions than the glamour fabrics. They range from the sheers (which we've already covered) to the lustrous sequined or metallic finishes.

Sequined fabrics: After cutting, catch ends of chain stitch with which sequin strips are sewn to fabric, either by hand or by stay-stitching on the machine.

Stitch slowly and keep extra needles close at hand. You may break a few. When it's necessary to remove some sequins (as at slide fastener seam allowances) cut through each sequin up to the hole only, and pull off. Do not cut retaining threads. Do not press.

Metallic brocades: Test the effect of heat on a sample fabric (some metallics may melt). Use warm, dry iron and press cloth, with light pressure, from the wrong side.

To keep the presser foot of your machine from slipping beneath the threads that 'float' over many metallic brocade surfaces, sew over strips of tissue paper.

Plaids, Checks and Stripes

SMALL plaids can be matched more easily than large ones: easy to work, they can be used for a greater variety of styles.

Even plaids have a balanced design on both lengthwise and crosswise directions. Unbalanced or uneven plaids are different in design in both lengthwise and crosswise directions—or different both up-and-down and across.

Stripes run in only one direction—lengthwise or crosswise—but may also be *even* or *uneven* in width.

Checks larger than ¼in should be matched at seamlines. Follow sewing guide for matching even plaids.

Patterns:

• When you choose a pattern for a plaid, choose one with simple design and few seams. Garments with a minimum number of pieces, designed with simple unbroken lines, give the best results.
• Check the pattern envelope to see if the design is illustrated in a plaid. If it is shown on the envelope, that is your go-ahead signal—the pattern will make up successfully in a plaid fabric.

Purchasing fabric:

• Matching plaid means some wastage, so buy more fabric than called for on the envelope. For average size plaids, adding an extra ¼ to ½ yard will be sufficient. For a large plaid, it would be wise to buy an extra ½ to 1 yard of fabric.

Layout:

• The finished look of your garment will depend on the way you arrange the plaid.
• Carefully plan the position of the most dominant lengthwise bar of the plaid. For best results place at the centre of the garment.
• Just below the shoulders place the most noticeable crosswise bar of plaid.
• Place hemlines on the lower edge of a complete block of plaid.
• When plaids are to be pleated, part of the design is folded in. Experiment by pinning up a piece of the plaid fabric in the suggested pleat width to get the best effect.

Cutting and marking:

• Before placing pattern pieces for cutting out, pin the layers of plaid together in both directions, along prominent stripes, so that the design matches exactly and will not shift when cutting.
• For a professionally matched plaid garment, use the pattern notches as your guides. Notches of corresponding pieces must be placed on the same lines of the plaid.
• Match seam lines not cutting lines, or you will lose the match when the seams are sewn.
• Important places to match a plaid jacket, dress or blouse are at the centre fronts and backs, and side seams from hem to underarm. (See diag 15, B-B.)

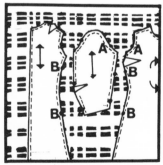

DIAGRAM 15

• Because of the front underarm dart, side seams cannot be matched their entire length.
• Matching at notches results in side seams being matched from underarm notch to waistline.
• Usually sleeve and armhole cannot be matched at both front and back if the underarm sleeves are matched.

With set-in sleeves match the sleeve front notch to the armhole front notch at the seam line (diag 15, A-A).

For kimono sleeves, match front and back below the notch on the shoulder seam.

• For a skirt, match all notches at side seams.

• For slacks, match the centre front, centre back and side seam notches (diag 16, C-C).

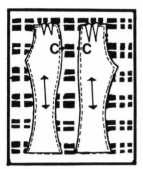

DIAGRAM 16

• Centre seams at front and back should always be matched the full length of a dress.

• Try to avoid placing darts on the most noticeable bar. Also try to plan a complete block to go around the lower edge.

Stripes

Striped fabrics are easier to handle than plaid fabrics because the design runs in only one direction—lengthwise or crosswise—and therefore need be matched or arranged in only one direction.

There are two types of stripes—*even* and *uneven*. No problem exists in cutting even stripes. You need only observe the ordinary precautions of laying matching parts on the same stripes.

Uneven stripes must be cut as you would cut a one-way fabric—with the tops of the pieces pointing in the same direction.

When working with uneven lengthwise stripes you may plan to arrange the stripes to move in opposite directions from the centre (a balanced effect) or to follow right around the figure.

For a *balanced* effect with an uneven lengthwise stripe you will need a centre front and back seam. Be sure to leave ⅝in seam allowance on pieces designed to be cut on the fold. On a single thickness of *reversible* fabric, place the centre seam lines on the dominant stripe.

When you want the stripe to follow right around the figure care must be taken when cutting the sleeves. When arranging uneven *lengthwise* stripes in set-in sleeves, make sure that the stripes of the sleeve move in the same direction as those in the bodice. Use the same stripe for the centre of the sleeves that you chose to place in the centre front and back. When using uneven *crosswise* stripes, let the stripes move down the bodice and skirt in their natural sequence. Then match the sleeve

stripes to the bodice stripes at the notches. If they cannot be matched at both back and front, match the front only.

Tips for a Good-Looking Garment

Seams and Seam Finishes

SEAMS and seam finishes are mostly determined by the fabric and their use on the garment. Standard seam allowance on patterns is ⅝in wide. Keep seams even, press seams as you work and clip curved seams at intervals before pressing.

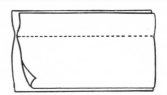

Plain Seam — most common on firm fabrics and lined coats. With right sides together stitch seam and press open.

DIAGRAM 1

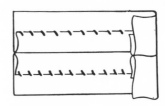

Overcast Seam — single for fabric edges that fray. Tack, stitch and press seam open. Overcast each edge, taking up about ⅛in.

DIAGRAM 2

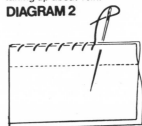

Overcast Seam — double for armholes, waistline seams: neaten together. Tack and stitch seam. Overcast edges together and press to one side.

DIAGRAM 3

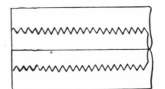

Pinked Seam — for non-frayable fabrics — wool, silk, velvet. After seam is stitched finish edges with pinking shears. Press seams open.

DIAGRAM 4

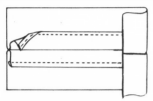

Machine Finished Edges — for non-bulky fabrics that ravel: stitch seam, turn and stitch raw edges, press seam open.

DIAGRAM 5

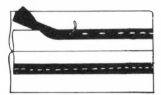

Bound Seams — for unlined jackets and coats: stitch and press seam open. Tack binding to cover each raw edge then stitch through all layers.

DIAGRAM 6

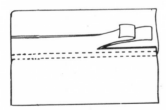

Double Stitched Seam — for sheer fabrics: stitch an ordinary seam. Make a second row of stitching close to the first. Trim close to second stitching.

DIAGRAM 7

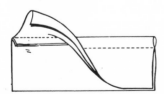

French Seam — for washable sheers. Wrong sides together make seam half depth of seam allowance. Trim close to stitching. Turn to wrong side, crease along seam and stitch encasing edges.

DIAGRAM 8

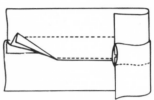

Flat Felled Seam: Stitch plain seam on right side. Trim one edge to within ⅛in from stitching. Turn in other edge and topstitch it over trimmed edge.

DIAGRAM 9

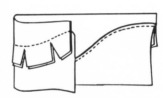

Topstitched Seam: For decoration. Stitch and press both edges to one side. Clip curved seam edges. Topstitch even distance from seam line on outside.

DIAGRAM 10

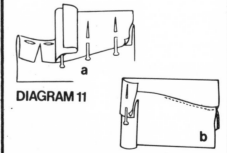

DIAGRAM 11

Lapped Seam: Turn under seam allowance of top piece and press. Match seamed edges on wrong side (a). Pin at right angles to folded edge (b). Topstitch close to turned edge on outside.

The All-Important Hem

ALL eyes will be focused on your hemline. Different skirts need different hems. (See diags 12 to 18.) For lightweight fabrics use the slip-stitched hem; for heavyweight fabrics or those that ravel easily use the taped hem. For firmly woven fabrics and knits use the catch-stitch hem.

To prepare:

Have hem marked with pins parallel to the floor. Turn up along pins, matching seams. Press, avoiding pins. Baste close to fold, taking pins out as you go. Mark depth of hem plus ¼in with chalk or pins. Trim surplus.

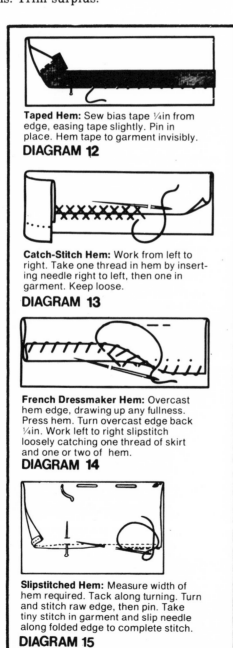

Taped Hem: Sew bias tape ¼in from edge, easing tape slightly. Pin in place. Hem tape to garment invisibly.

DIAGRAM 12

Catch-Stitch Hem: Work from left to right. Take one thread in hem by inserting needle right to left, then one in garment. Keep loose.

DIAGRAM 13

French Dressmaker Hem: Overcast hem edge, drawing up any fullness. Press hem. Turn overcast edge back ¼in. Work left to right slipstitch loosely catching one thread of skirt and one or two of hem.

DIAGRAM 14

Slipstitched Hem: Measure width of hem required. Tack along turning. Turn and stitch raw edge, then pin. Take tiny stitch in garment and slip needle along folded edge to complete stitch.

DIAGRAM 15

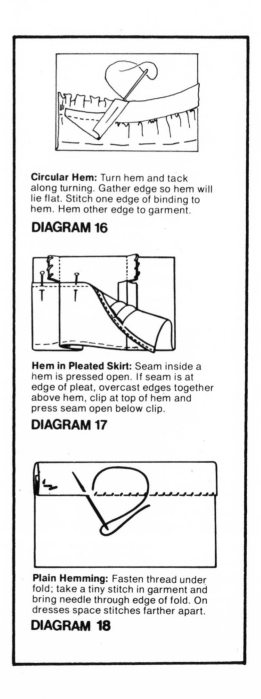

Circular Hem: Turn hem and tack along turning. Gather edge so hem will lie flat. Stitch one edge of binding to hem. Hem other edge to garment.

DIAGRAM 16

Hem in Pleated Skirt: Seam inside a hem is pressed open. If seam is at edge of pleat, overcast edges together above hem, clip at top of hem and press seam open below clip.

DIAGRAM 17

Plain Hemming: Fasten thread under fold; take a tiny stitch in garment and bring needle through edge of fold. On dresses space stitches farther apart.

DIAGRAM 18

Even stripes in which the colour and width of stripes are repeated consecutively, either lengthwise or crosswise of the fabric, are easy to work with.

Lace is a delightful fabric so choose a simple pattern which will accentuate the beauty of the material.

The depth of the hem and the method of stitching depend on the garment and type of fabric.

Buttons and Buttonholes

BUTTONS are styling touches that make a big difference. They deserve careful thought and careful sewing, too. It's wise to buy a button comparable in size to the one sketched on the pattern envelope, since it is the designer's choice and will fit the buttonholes marked on the pattern. Buttons should slip through the buttonhole easily and smoothly.

Buttonholes are usually ⅛in longer than the diameter of the button. A button 1⅛in diameter needs a 1¼in buttonhole. There are, however, some exceptions to this. One is when very small buttons are used; then the difference would be less. Another is when a thick or heavy fabric is used for a coat and the button is covered in the same fabric. Then a slightly larger buttonhole would be needed. It is a good idea to make a test buttonhole for a thick button on a scrap of the fabric. Cut a slit in the fabric the diameter of the button and increase the length of the opening until the button slips through easily. Use this measurement for the buttonhole on the garment.

Types of buttonholes

There are two kinds of buttonholes, bound and worked. Bound buttonholes have the edges finished with fabric; worked buttonholes have the edges finished with thread. Those parts of the garment where buttonholes are used should be interfaced for firmness and strength. Stitching must begin and end exactly on lines indicating the ends of the buttonholes.

Worked buttonholes may be done by machine or by hand. Machine made buttonholes save many hours of work and are satisfactory for most garments. Hand worked buttonholes have an eyelet at the end of the buttonhole, this tailored buttonhole is used on men's clothing and top coats. Mark the buttonhole and punch a hole at the outer end with a stiletto. Cut on line for buttonhole and overcast edges of buttonhole and eyelet. For extra strength work the buttonhole stitches over a cord and finish the inner end with a bar tack. A corded buttonhole will also wear better than a buttonhole made without it. Work over the edges with buttonhole or blanket stitches keeping them close together. If you insert the stiletto from the right side every few stitches it will help to keep the fabric turned under making it easier to shape the eyelet and work the buttonhole stitches.

Placing buttonholes and buttons

Patterns clearly mark buttonhole locations and sizes with a printed line. If, however, you have lengthened or shortened your pattern you must respace the buttonholes. On a bodice, keep the top buttonhole in its position on the pattern so that the neckline closure is not changed. Also keep the lowest buttonhole where it is relative to the waistline and belt. Then evenly space the remaining buttonholes between the top and bottom ones. On a skirt that buttons down the front, keep the top buttonhole in position relative to the waistline and the bottom one as it is in relation to the hem; respace others evenly between these two buttonholes.

On garments that close at centre front, the horizontal buttonholes usually extend ⅛in over the centre line towards the outer edge. (See

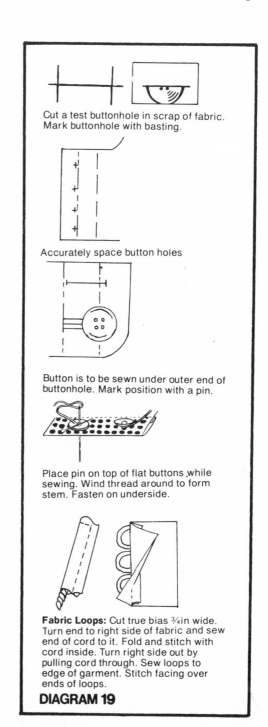

Cut a test buttonhole in scrap of fabric. Mark buttonhole with basting.

Accurately space button holes

Button is to be sewn under outer end of buttonhole. Mark position with a pin.

Place pin on top of flat buttons while sewing. Wind thread around to form stem. Fasten on underside.

Fabric Loops: Cut true bias ¾in wide. Turn end to right side of fabric and sew end of cord to it. Fold and stitch with cord inside. Turn right side out by pulling cord through. Sew loops to edge of garment. Stitch facing over ends of loops.

DIAGRAM 19

Buttons should be given careful thought and careful sewing as they are styling touches that can make a big difference to a garment.

diag 19 for marking buttonholes and buttons.) Coat buttonholes extend ¼in over the centre line. Vertical buttonholes are placed on the centre line.

Buttons used with the horizontal buttonholes are sewn on the underwrap in line with the buttonhole and exactly on the centre front or

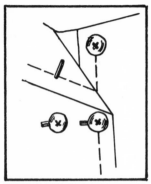

DIAGRAM 20

back line (diag 20). If the buttonhole is vertical, mark the upper end on the underwrap and sew the button ⅛in below this mark. When the closing is an off-centre one or the buttonhole is slanted, place top wrap over underwrap; match centres. For off-centre closings put a pin through the end of the buttonhole nearest the edge if it is horizontal or through the upper end if it is vertical. Centre of button is placed ⅛in from pin—away from the outer edge if horizontal, down from top if vertical. If the buttonhole is slanted, put the pin through the end nearer the outer edge, and place the button ⅛in from the pin. If the buttonhole slants *up* towards the edge, the button goes ⅛in from the top of the buttonhole (diag 21); if it slants *down* towards the edge, ⅛in from the bottom of the buttonhole (diag 22).

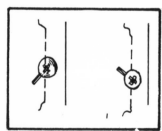

DIAGRAM 21 22

Buttonhole making is easy if you have a modern sewing machine—neat, accurate buttonholes of every size can be made with a minimum of effort.

How to change the size of buttonholes

Vertical buttonholes may easily be lengthened or shortened for use with larger or smaller buttons. This is done at the lower end of the buttonhole. To make a horizontal buttonhole smaller, simply shorten from the inner end until it is ⅛in longer than the button size you plan to use. Sometimes a difficulty may arise when you try to use larger buttons with horizontal buttonholes as the

buttonhole length is tied in with the width of the underlap and the facing.

Never lengthen a buttonhole so far inward that it extends beyond the edge of the underlap or the facing; nor extend a buttonhole too close to the outer edge as the edge of the button should be at least ⅜in from the opening.

If the buttonhole needs to be lengthened only ⅛in or ¼in, it may be done easily by extending both ends of the marked buttonhole one half the extra amount ($^1/_{16}$ or ⅛in). If this cannot be done you will need to make a wider underlap. However, you must decide to do this before cutting out the garment so that the underlap can be cut wider.

Remember: On lightweight fabrics and children's clothes, the width of the underlap is only a few inches so do not increase the button size more than ⅛in beyond the size suggested on the pattern.

Button shanks or stems

Buttons should not be sewn down flat to the garment with firm thread; there should always be a shank or stem to allow the button to ride smoothly in the buttonhole when it is buttoned.

Some buttons come equipped with their own shank (see diag 23), others may not (see the tunnel button, diag 24).

 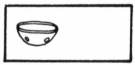

DIAGRAM 23   **DIAGRAM 24**

To add a shank to a button, make a stitch on the right side of the fabric where the button is to be sewn. Bring the needle through the button. Then place a pin or match across the top to allow for extra 'play'. Continue sewing back and forth over the pin (diag 25) in any way desired (see f··· suggested ways in diag 26). Remove the pin

DIAGRAM 25

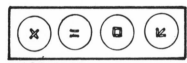

DIAGRAM 26

and wind the thread firmly around the threads under the button, forming the shank. Draw the needle to the wrong side of the fabric and fasten the thread with several stitches to make it absolutely secure. (See diags 27, 28 for bound and worked buttonholes.)

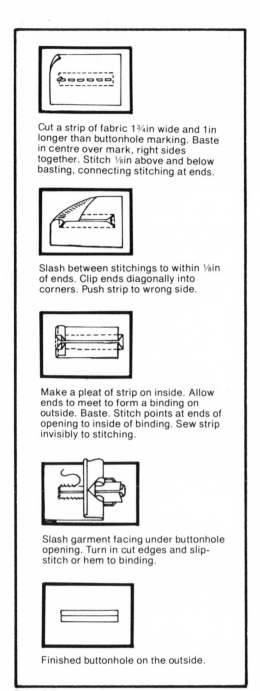

Cut a strip of fabric 1¾in wide and 1in longer than buttonhole marking. Baste in centre over mark, right sides together. Stitch ⅛in above and below basting, connecting stitching at ends.

Slash between stitchings to within ⅛in of ends. Clip ends diagonally into corners. Push strip to wrong side.

Make a pleat of strip on inside. Allow ends to meet to form a binding on outside. Baste. Stitch points at ends of opening to inside of binding. Sew strip invisibly to stitching.

Slash garment facing under buttonhole opening. Turn in cut edges and slip-stitch or hem to binding.

Finished buttonhole on the outside.

DIAGRAM 27

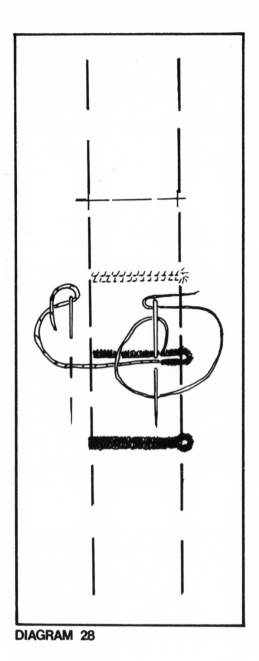

DIAGRAM 28

Sleeve Finishes

THERE are several ways of finishing a long sleeve. One way is with a continuous placket which can also be used for the back closing of a child's dress and the opening in a gathered skirt. Others are puffed sleeve with elastic inserted, and sleeve with turned-back cuff.

The continuous placket:

1. Stitch on the marked slanted lines of the sleeve opening. Slash through centre between stitching (diag 29).

DIAGRAM 29

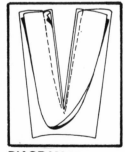

DIAGRAM 30

2. Cut a straight grain strip 2in wide and twice the slash length. Stitch to right side of opening (diag 30).

3. Turn in raw edges of lap, then topstitch turned edges over the seam (diag 31).

DIAGRAM 31

4. Turn the lap to wrong side and press. Stitch the two sides together diagonally at the point (diag 32).

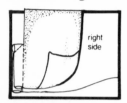

DIAGRAM 32

5. The finished placket from the right side (diag 33).

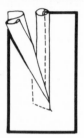

DIAGRAM 33

Puffed sleeve with elastic:
Finish lower edge with hem or facing wide enough for elastic. Leave opening at underarm seam. Edge-stitch the lower edge. Insert elastic; lap and sew ends together securely (diag 34).

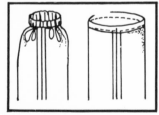

DIAGRAM 34

Sleeve with turned-back cuff:
Method a: Stitch right side of cuff to wrong side of sleeve, matching seams. Fold cuff to outside; turn under the free edge of cuff. Fold cuff over and hem free edge to seam stitching. Turn cuff to outside and tack edge to underarm seam of sleeve (diag 35).

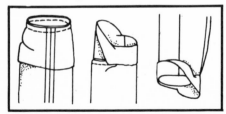

DIAGRAM 35

Method b: Make cuff. Whip-stitch ends together and baste to lower edge of sleeve on outside. Baste bias on top of cuff, joining bias ends. Stitch. Turn under free edge of bias and hem over seam on inside. Turn cuff over sleeve (diag 36).

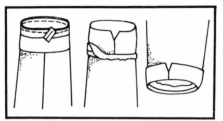

DIAGRAM 36

How to set in a sleeve

Follow the directions given in diag 37 for a professional result every time.

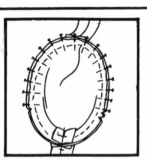

With wrong side of garment towards you, set sleeve in, matching notches and underarm seams. Pin sleeve to armhole easing in fullness across top.

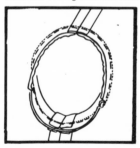

Tack and stitch sleeve in armhole.

Place top of sleeve over your tailors cushion and press through a damp cloth. Shrink out any fullnesss in sleeve cap by pressing sleeve and armhole seams together from sleeve side. Overcast.

DIAGRAM 37

Sleeves can be given interest with cuffs and a nice fashion effect is achieved with matching cuffs and shirt pockets.

Collars and Necklines

NECKLINE treatments can turn an otherwise plain garment into an interesting one. Necklines may be finished with collars (see diag 38 for attaching a collar with bias) or with facing if the garment is collarless (diags 39, 40, 41).

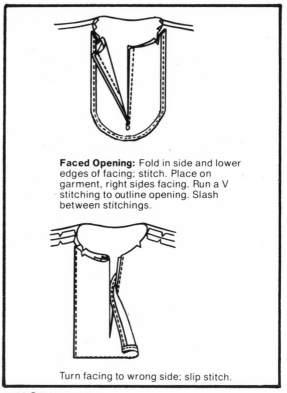

Faced Opening: Fold in side and lower edges of facing; stitch. Place on garment, right sides facing. Run a V stitching to outline opening. Slash between stitchings.

Turn facing to wrong side; slip stitch.

DIAGRAM 39

Pin collar and facing with right sides together. Tack and stitch around outside edge. Trim seam.

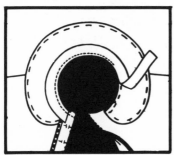

Turn collar to right side, tack edge and press. Tack collar to garment on right side. Turn under seam allowance on front lap of garment. Next turn under-lap hem allowance back over ends of collar; pin. Tack bias to neck edge extending ends over the hem. Stitch in position.

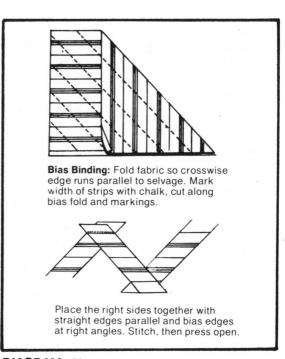

Bias Binding: Fold fabric so crosswise edge runs parallel to selvage. Mark width of strips with chalk, cut along bias fold and markings.

Place the right sides together with straight edges parallel and bias edges at right angles. Stitch, then press open.

DIAGRAM 40

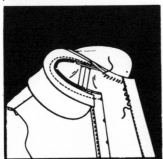

Turn the hems and facing to inside. Fold bias strip over turnings, sew in position. Blind-tack hems in place.

DIAGRAM 38

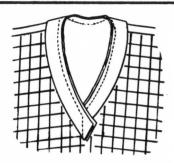 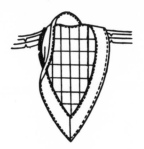

Bias Facing for V-Neck: Stitch 1½in width bias strip to neck edge, right sides together. Begin and end strip at point of V. Stitch ends at point.

Trim away surplus bias strip at point and press seam open there.

Turn facing to inside of garment. Baste and stitch along turning. Turn raw edge and stitch, leave edge free and catch down only at shoulder seams.

DIAGRAM 41

The collar is one of the most important parts of any garment, and must fit well. Accessories at the neckline can add interest to a plain garment.

Pleats form folds in the fabric and give fullness and shape to a garment.

Pleats in Skirts

DIRECTIONS for making skirts with pleats are given in the pattern together with all necessary markings. Be sure to follow directions carefully. The simpler types of pleats which can be made by the home dressmaker are:

Straight or knife: Pleats all turning in one direction. They should lap from right to left (diag 42).

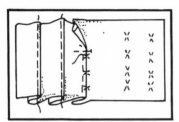

DIAGRAM 42

Box pleats: Two straight pleats turned away from each other (diag 43).

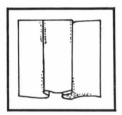

DIAGRAM 43

Inverted pleats: Two straight pleats turned towards each other (diag 44).

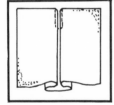

DIAGRAM 44

Kick pleats: A single knife or inverted pleat in a seam to give more walking room in a slim skirt. If a skirt with kick pleat must be lengthened or shortened, make the alteration in the pattern *above* the pleat to retain its original length.

Marking and making

In a large area, such as a skirt, transfer pleat lines from pattern to fabric (diag 45).

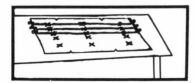

DIAGRAM 45

Working on right side, bring markings indicating the fold to the next line of markings. Pin and baste in place; press lightly (diag 46). Stitch as

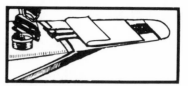

DIAGRAM 46

indicated by pattern; remove basting; press well.

In a small area, such as the front of a blouse, pleats may be put in without marking fabric.

Pin pattern to fabric through all lines of pleat marking. Fold pattern and fabric together in pleats; pin in place and press lightly to make pleat lines. Remove pattern and baste pleats in place.

Hems in pleated skirts

Pleated skirts should be hemmed before pleats are put in to make sure the lower edge is a straight, on-grain line. If shortening is needed after the hem is in and pleats made, it is done at the skirt top.

Stitching pleats

Always stitch pleats from the bottom up. Stitching down may stretch the fabric.

In fabrics that do not retain a press well, it is a good idea to edge-stitch the under fold of the pleats. Edge-stitching may also be done as a decoration on the outer edges (diag 47).

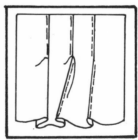

DIAGRAM 47

Inserting a Slide Fastener

IF you follow diag 48 carefully, you'll find the plain seam system is easiest every time.

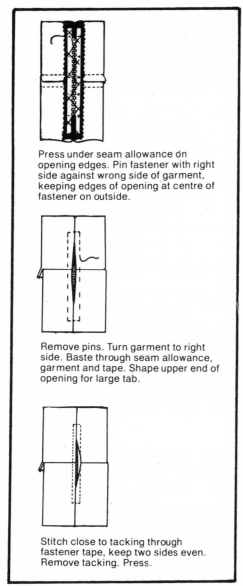

Press under seam allowance on opening edges. Pin fastener with right side against wrong side of garment, keeping edges of opening at centre of fastener on outside.

Remove pins. Turn garment to right side. Baste through seam allowance, garment and tape. Shape upper end of opening for large tab.

Stitch close to tacking through fastener tape, keep two sides even. Remove tacking. Press.

DIAGRAM 48

Making a Patch Pocket

PATCH pockets are fashionable. There are many shapes and sizes but the general method of making and attaching to the garment is the same.

Making plain patch pockets:
1. At top edge, turn ¼in to inside and stitch (diag 49).
2. Turn top edge to outside on fold line to form hem facing. Starting at top of hem facing, stitch around pocket on seam line (diag 50).

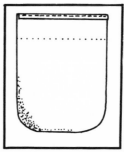

DIAGRAM 49

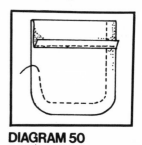

DIAGRAM 50

3. Trim corners of hem facing and seam allowance. Clip curves in 'V' up to the stitching (diag 51).
4. Turn hem facing to inside and press. Press seam allowance to inside (diag 52).

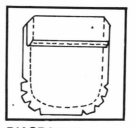

DIAGRAM 51

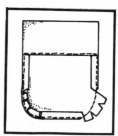

DIAGRAM 52

Attaching patch pocket to garment:
There are two ways to attach a patch pocket to the garment. Pin in place and, if necessary, baste. Then:
1. Topstitch in place close to pocket edge, reinforcing top corners (diag 53) OR

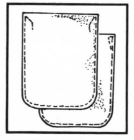

DIAGRAM 53

2. Turn garment to wrong side and with small backstitches sew through wrong side of both garment and pocket. Be careful stitches do not show on right side of pocket. This is a very good way if the pocket is on a coat and the material is heavy.

When applying a patch pocket in a matching fabric be sure to cut the fabric so that it will match the fabric design on the garment at the place where the pocket is to be applied.

Tricks of Tailoring

IF you're planning to sew one of the new soft suits, one of the new-length jackets, remember that this type of garment needs an extra something—tailoring.

In making any tailored garment your first consideration is the shrinkage of the fabric. Unless it is marked pre-shrunk you would be wise to shrink all fabrics before using them.

Wet a strip of sheeting the length and width of your fabric. Place this on your material and roll them together, the sheet inside.

Leave for two to eight hours, or overnight, before removing the sheet.

Press the damp fabric with a hot iron over a dry pressing cloth. Your fabric should be face downwards and press slowly working straight down the grain, never diagonally.

Do not allow the iron to rest for long in one place. It may imprint the fabric. Continue pressing until fabric is dry.

Underlining and interfacing will make all the difference to your garments.

Underlining fabric, which is cut from the same pattern pieces as the outer fabric, improves the look of any garment. Choose a weight of underlining that is not too heavy for the outer fabric or it will spoil the line. For jackets and vests, unbleached muslin is perfect.

Interfacing used between the facing and outer fabrics gives shape to fronts, collars, lapels and edges.

Woven materials, such as canvas, have a lengthwise and crosswise grain. Non-woven linings are fibres pressed together and have no grain and may be used in any direction.

Front interfacings are stitched to the seam lines of the garment pieces.

Slip-stitch bias strips of interfacing to the hemlines of cuffs and jacket bottoms to form edges and hold the shape.

Always stitch seams in the direction shown by arrows on your pattern. In this way you are sewing with the grain and you prevent wobbly, taut or puckered seams.

Test the grain by running your finger down the cut edge of a seam. If the edge remains flat you are moving in the direction of the grain. If the threads ruffle, you are moving against the grain.

If the seam is curved, sew in the direction in which you can follow the grain line longest.

One of the most important areas of professional tailoring is the care taken with seams.

Before stitching, clip interfacing ¼in away from the corners.

After stitching, clip away seam allowances of interfacings to the seam line.

Trim other seam allowances so that the bulk of the seam is layered and evenly distributed.

Clip away excess fabric where seams cross and be sure to trim fabric away at corners to make a sharp point.

Always press as you sew, using a steam iron.

Just before stitching the lining into the jacket, press the whole garment carefully from the right side, using a well-padded board and pressing cloth to avoid putting a shine on the fabric.

To get the smooth rounded top to sleeves, cut a 2in strip of soft woollen fabric on the bias or a piece of non-woven interlining. Fold the strip in half lengthwise and stitch it in with the sleeve between the notches, folded edge towards the sleeve (diag 54).

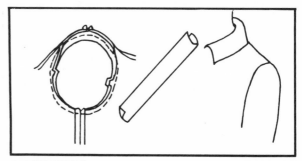

DIAGRAM 54

Clip and layer seam allowance then press firmly, but lightly, into the top of the sleeve.

Lining covers the inside seams. Use lining fabrics that agree with cleaning rules for outer fabrics.

Shrinkage percentage should also agree. We have all had the experience at some time or other when the lining has shrunk and ruined the shape of a favourite garment. (See diag 55 for placement of lining in a skirt; diag 56 for lining in sleeves; diag 57 for lining in a jacket.)

DIAGRAM 56

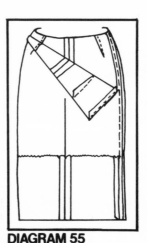

DIAGRAM 55

DIAGRAM 57

Well-tailored casual clothes can be flattering to most figures.

How to Interface A Vest

undisturbed until all steam is gone, the crease thoroughly set.

Press with grain line and with the nap of fabric. Never press across a hem—always with the lengthwise thread of the grain. (See diag 60.)

ONE trick to sewing a perfect vest is to trim all the outside edges—those encased seams or faced edges that fold back on themselves and tend to be very bulky. These seams often include a third layer of fabric, an interfacing, and to reduce the bulk, seams are layered or staggered so that there will be no sudden 'jump off' of thickness. Instead, the thickness will gradually taper off. A good guide line for the layering of seams is to trim the interfacing to ⅛in, one edge of the fabric to ¼in, the remaining edge to a scant ⅜in.

For a neat, flat corner, reduce the bulk even further by diagonally trimming the seam allowances close to the stitching lines on both sides of the point.

A quick and easy way to add the body of an interfacing without actually interfacing a vest is to use a bonding material (available in narrow strips or by the yard on a paper backing) which adds stiffness. This technique is especially good for adding body to the lower front corners of vests.

After you have pinned the lining, or facing, to the vest, cut bonding to the desired size and pin in corners and along front edges so it will be included in the seam as you stitch (diag 58). Layer seams and trim corners as indicated in diag 59. Turn vest to the right side and press firmly with an iron as indicated on the bonding material directions.

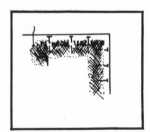

DIAGRAM 58   **DIAGRAM 59**

How to Press

USE strips of tissue paper in seams and facings to prevent imprints from showing on right side of garments and to set the crease in the pleats.

For setting knife-edge crease on pleats or slacks, insert a strip of tissue paper and fold over the edge of each pleat.

Use a press cloth and proceed to steam press. If possible leave the garment on the board

Press each seam as you sew. This is essential to allow other seamed pieces to lie flat when joined.

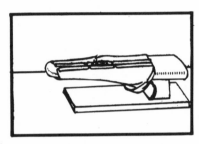

Press sleeves on sleeve board for perfect results. Use board also when pressing awkward seams and small darts.

Use a small brush to open seams. Press over a dry cloth or a slightly dampened cloth. This is especially good for wool.

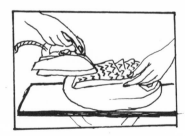

Use a tailor's cushion for pressing armhole seams and shrinking out the fullness at the top of sleeves. (To make a cushion, stitch two 12in ovals together and stuff with wadding until very firm.)

DIAGRAM 60

Stripes are a perennial favourite and not only do they produce interesting effects but they can also create flattering illusions.

For tailored clothes wool is a good selection since it shapes and shrinks so beautifully, and will not shine readily when pressed.

Pay special attention to the finishing touches and you will have a professional-looking garment like this one.

The Finishing Touches

TO help you stitch better and to sew the most for your money, keep abreast of all the latest developments and discoveries in the sewing world, and brush up on techniques that fashion brings to the fore.

You will find many advances in sewing machines. In the modern ranges, machines will do fancy stitches, tacking and buttonholes, with stitch selectors adjustable for every fabric. Some convert to free-arm for sewing those intricate parts on collars, cuffs, sleeves, legs of pants and children's clothes.

How to Gather the Waist of a Dress

THERE are three ways to get pretty gathers at the waistline of a one-piece dress: by inserting elastic into a casing; by stitching elastic directly to the dress; by using elastic thread.

When the pattern you choose specifies the casing method, the casing will be either an actual pattern piece or a strip of bias tape. For this type of gathering, insert 'heavy-duty' or 'strong stretch' rayon elastic into the casing. The pattern will indicate the width needed.

Elastic in a casing often tends to 'roll' or bunch gathers in spots. To avoid this and to have good distribution of fullness, place four vertical lines of stitching to anchor the elastic, through the elastic and the garment (the length of these stitching lines should be the same as the width of the elastic used). Place two rows of stitches in the back and two in front.

To avoid fullness in the centre front, gathers can be distributed to either side of the centre front of the garment and held by these anchoring stitches—each midway between the centre front and a side seam.

When you plan to shirr an area of a dress by stitching elastic directly to the garment, purchase elastic that is a combination of nylon and rubber, the width indicated in the pattern. This elastic has a softer stretch than rayon elastic and is easier to sew on. It is sometimes called 'lingerie' elastic and gives the best results in this type of shirring.

Mark the stitching lines on the wrong side of the garment. Cut the length of elastic specified in the pattern, divide the elastic and the stitching line into quarters or eighths, depending upon the length of the area to be shirred. Allow ½in of elastic at each end for finishing.

Pin the elastic to the garment stitching line at these points. Stitch, either with a zigzag stitch or a large straight stitch (8-10 stitches to the inch). Stretch the elastic between pins as you go, using both hands, stretching both in front of and in back of the presser foot. Fasten elastic ends securely (diag 1).

DIAGRAM 1

DIAGRAM 2

Another way to gather fabric is with elastic thread. This method is pretty when you wish several rows of close-together shirring.

Select a 10-12 stitch length. Wind the elastic thread by hand on to the bobbin. Use mercerised cotton for the top thread. Be sure to test the fullness on a swatch of your fabric since each fabric reacts differently.

Mark the first stitching line with basting. Stitch on the *right* side of the garment (so the elastic thread will be on the wrong side). When you stitch additional rows, hold the fabric already shirred flat, by stretching it both in front and in back of the presser foot (diag 2). Spacing of rows may be judged by the edge of the presser foot. At the end, tie elastic and needle threads together.

How to Finish Sleeveless Garments

TO give shape, body and a smooth line to a sleeveless armhole, it must be interfaced and understitched.

Use the facing pattern for the interfacing (the facing and interfacing can be cut out at the same time). Stitch the underarm seam of the armhole interfacing, press open, and baste the interfacing to the armhole edge on the wrong side of the bodice.

Construct the armhole facing. Machine stitch ¼in from the outer edge. To finish this edge, pink, hand overcast, machine zigzag or turn and stitch. A pretty, and personal, touch is to finish the facing edges with lace or trimming. Pin and stitch the facing to the armhole edge, right sides together, matching notches and underarm seams.

Trim the interfacing close to the line of stitching. Trim facing to within ¼in of the seam line, and clip at intervals along the curves. To hold the facing neatly in place, understitch it by stitching on the right side of the facing, very close to the seam line, through the facing and the seam allowances (diag 3). The facing will turn easily

and lie flat. Trim interfacing even with the finished edge of the facing. Press and slip-stitch to the underarm and shoulder seams.

Topstitching

TOPSTITCHING is a distinctive detail currently decorating dresses with bold, curving seams, and sharply tailored garments. You can add topstitching to a garment either by machine or hand.

Choose a heavy thread of the same type as the fabric. If you are topstitching cotton or linen, use heavy-duty. If you are topstitching silk or wool, or linen that will not be washed, use silk twist (remember that silk dyes aren't always colourfast to hot water).

To topstitch by machine on wool or silk, or linen to be dry cleaned, put silk twist in the upper threading of your sewing machine. You need not waste it in the bobbin as it will not show. Use a size 16 needle (which will take the thicker thread). Loosen the top tension a bit, so that no part of the bobbin thread will show through on the top, and use a long stitch. If you find that silk twist will not go through the top threading of your machine, put it in the bobbin and do your topstitching from the wrong side of the garment.

If you are working on cotton fabric, sew two rows of heavy-duty thread right on top of each other. This will give the appearance of one row of somewhat heavier thread.

Topstitching by hand is called hand-picking. Baste the line to be stitched with fine thread.

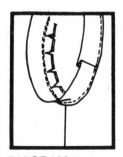

DIAGRAM 3

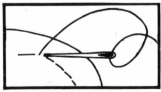

DIAGRAM 4

On this stitching line, bring needle through to the surface from underneath, take a backstitch, picking up approximately one yarn of fabric. Bring needle forward and up through fabric about ½in from the backstitch. Continue with a backstitch, then forward (diag 4) until you have finished.

Adding Special Trims

Gathered lace trim is easy to make this way. Put buttonhole twist in your bobbin; use the longest basting stitch. After stitching the length of lace to be gathered, tie the thread ends at one end of the lace into a loop and slip it over the sewing machine spindle. Back away from the machine, lace in hand, until it is taut. Then, pulling on the bobbin thread, push lace up into the gathered length you wish and proceed exactly as the pattern tells you.

Rhinestones by the yard come slipped on to twill tape. The double and triple rows are best used on straight areas. The single row is pliable enough for curved areas.

When working with this tape, cut it about 1in longer than you need. Slip off ½in of rhinestones at either end and tuck the excess tape under the rhinestones as you attach them, by hand, stitching through the tape between each one of the stones.

Feathers are attached to a finished dress. Mark the feather line with thread tracing. Then, working from the wrong side, slip-stitch through the fabric and around the 'spine' of the feathers. This way you won't have to wander through feathers looking for spine and stitchline.

Picot edging is easy to use and adds a pretty finish to a lace dress. Press hems of sleeves and skirt. Trim away all but ¼in, baste the edging to the skirt of the dress, covering the raw hem edge, with the picot edging peeking out. Machine stitch.

Glitter by the yard: When adding glitter by the yard to a finished garment slip-stitch it first along the outer curve of an area, then ease it in on the inner curve.

Finish off ends by removing jewels from the seam allowance area and turning under before stitching in place.

Fringe: This can be inserted into seams by machine very easily. It needs care, as it has a tendency to come off its woven binding.

Stabilise the cut end with ordinary adhesive tape as soon as you cut it to avoid this happening.

If you find fringe becomes tangled or gets in your way as you sew, place tissue paper over it as you work. It can easily be torn away when you have finished.

Adding Ribbons and Braids

A NEAT mitred corner is often the difference in a professional or a non-professional trim. When you trim a skirt with embroidered ribbon or a wide braid trim, and must turn a corner, the trims must be mitred, as they have no 'give'.

Stitch trim, on both sides, down to the corner. Then fold ribbon back on itself and to the side, making a right angle. Press to make a diagonal crease on wrong side. Stitch along the diagonal crease through ribbon and garment. Then stitch along edges to the next corner.

An easy way to get rickrack attached in a straight line is to draw a guideline with a pencil on the right side of the fabric (the marks will be covered). Roll the rickrack up on a pencil and begin stitching the loose end in place, with a straight line of stitching through the middle of the rickrack. As you stitch, unroll it a bit at a time. This method keeps you from having a tangled mass of rickrack in your lap.

For an instant scalloped edge, apply scalloped braid in much the same way as you apply rickrack, stitching straight across braid at edge away from scallop.

There's a trick to sewing grosgrain ribbon on without puckering—which it is apt to do. Baste it in place with diagonal stitches (which hold more securely than running stitches). When stitching in place, sew both edges in the same direction. This will keep it flat and eliminate puckering that may occur if it is stitched down one side and up the other.

If the garment to be trimmed will be washed, remember to pre-wash both fabric and trim, as they may have different degrees of shrinkage.

How to Applique

APPLIQUES add a touch of colourful whimsy to fashion. They're meant to be fun.

When you work with appliques, let your imagination take over. Today's fun fashion appliques know no bounds where colour and design are concerned. There are patterns you can choose that

A coloured trim adds a gay note to a casual outfit.

have bold and imaginative applique transfers. You can try your hand at drawing your own, or cut applique designs from decorator prints.

Choose fabrics that do not fray easily. Non-woven fabrics, such as leathers and felts, are excellent. However, if you want the appliqued garment to be washable, choose appliques that match the garment fabric for best results.

A new way to get around the fraying problem and a way to add a bit of body to the applique at the same time, is to press the fabric you'll use to iron-on interfacing before you cut out your applique pictures.

Applique pictures that have no seam allowance are attached along the edge, to the ground fabric. An attractive, easy and much-used method of attaching appliques is with a satin stitch done by hand or machine.

By hand, satin stitching consists of passing thread over and under the applique and ground fabric in close parallel lines along the edge, keeping the width of the stitches precisely the same as you proceed around the applique (diag 5). The

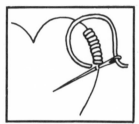

DIAGRAM 5

width of your satin stitch border can vary with the size of the applique. A width of ⅛in to ¼in is good.

Satin stitching can be easily and quickly done on a zigzag sewing machine. Baste the applique securely in place before you begin. Set the zigzag to a fine stitch and attach the applique along the edge (diag 6).

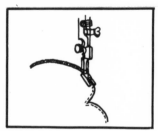

DIAGRAM 6

Appliqueing lace

Lace is the loveliest and most fascinating of fabrics. Some are bonded and these are sewn as any other opaque fabric. The newest ones have bolder designs and need slightly different handling. Some have large open motifs which are more hole than fabric.

These must have a sheer backing and, wherever

possible, the motif should be used for the edges at hem, neckline and sleeve. In some instances sleeve edges and hem can be cut to shape around the motifs, but the neckline must be appliqued or bound.

Sheer lace must be backed with flesh-coloured sheer and stitched over strips of tissue paper to prevent seams from puckering and to give you something more than holes for the needle to stitch on. Tear tissue away. Stitch again ⅛in inside seam allowance, then trim the seam allowance away to the second stitchline.

For applique lace borders around curved hemlines and necklines (diag 7), first determine your

DIAGRAM 7

hem and mark it with a line of basting.

Cut the scalloped border from the lace, leaving an excess of about ½in at the top beyond the end of the border design. Place the scalloped edge of the border along the basted hemline, curving it to fit the hem. Baste in place. Over-sew along the thick thread at the edge of the motif with tiny stitches. Press carefully.

Cut away excess lace along the top edge of the border. Turn dress to the wrong side and cut away all the extra fabric up to the hand-stitched line.

It takes time and attention to tailor clothes well, but the extra effort will be worthwhile when you proudly wear a high quality garment you have made for yourself.

Part 2

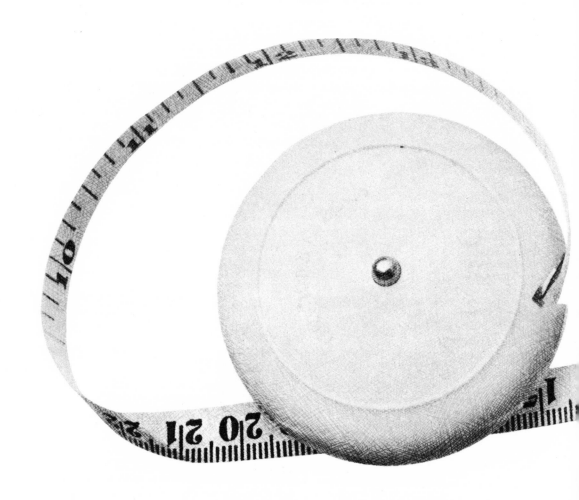

The Home Decorator's Touch

Decorating and furnishing your own home can be fun especially when you know how to sew. New curtains, new chair covers, a pillow case, a bedspread, colourful cushions and any number of other small items can change the personality and appearance of a room. But these home furnishings can be a costly item in any household budget; they are expensive to buy or to have professionally made. With time and patience and the basics of sewing knowledge you can do them successfully at home.

Sewing for Your Home

FURNISHINGS are a major item in any home, so it is the wise woman who sews for her home today. Not only does she save money, for made-to-order furnishings are expensive, but she can have the choice of colour, design and fabric content in the wide range of fabrics available.

Fabrics

One of the most exciting departments in any store for the homemaker is the fabric section. Here the wide variety of natural and man-made fibres, weaves, textures, special finishes, patterns and colours is almost endless. There is something for every type of home, for every room in it and for every use.

These fabrics can be sewn on your sewing machine without any problems. Look for pre-shrunk fabrics with guaranteed colour fastness so that your covers will look well all their working lives. Stretch covers are the newest fabrics on the market and are ideal for slipcovers where a close fit is needed. Vinyls may be used for covers, especially for outdoor furniture or for chunky cushions in children's rooms.

Fabrics used for decorating in homes with growing youngsters should be firm and sturdy to stand up to lots of hard wear and sometimes rough usage. Practically any washing fabric can be used for decorating rooms for children. Strong denims, cottons, sailcloths, ginghams, corduroy, mattress tickings, burlaps, are all effective when used in children's rooms. They will stand a lot of washing. Many of the drip-dry finishes need little or no ironing. Some of the newest fabrics have a permanent water and stain repellent finish that saves many a dry cleaning bill or permanent stain.

When decorating girls' rooms other materials can be added to the list: polished cottons, chintz, dress fabrics, such as crisp, fadeless cottons and ginghams.

There are also crisp sheers, organdies and nylons —plain, flocked and embroidered. These fabrics are best washed by hand and hung out to dry almost dripping wet. Silks and other luxurious furnishing fabrics belong in homes where there are no small children.

When choosing fabrics with any kind of design, especially a large one, it may be necessary to buy extra yardage to make it possible to centre the large design in slipcovers and curtains. How frequently the design is repeated and whether or not a design has a one-way direction are also matters to be considered when buying patterned fabrics. Plain fabrics and those with an all-over design are the easiest for beginners to use, because there is no problem of matching. Small designs can often be used with plain fabric in matching colours for an interesting striped effect.

While most of today's fabrics for home decorating can be washed or cleaned not all are guaranteed against fading. So wherever possible choose sun-fast fabrics, especially in rooms that receive a lot of sun. Look among the dress fabrics for guaranteed fadeless fabrics for curtains, cloths and bedcovers. The 36in width can be used very successfully for any of these. For furniture exposed to sun choose fabrics in pale tones, yellows, ivories, golds, sand tones and whites—the fading of these colours will be barely noticeable.

Equipment

In sewing for your home do not forget that you are contributing your own time and effort. They are valuable and deserving of the best assistance in the way of equipment and supplies. The modern sewing machine is a boon to the home sewer with its variety of attachments that make the tedious jobs easier. Choose one that has a piping foot attachment, it will save hours of work. Embroidery attachments make it possible to give a professional look to table cloths and place mats. Try to have clear working space to the left when working with your machine.

You will also need good sharp scissors, a handy size is 7in to 8in from tip to handle with handles large enough for the fingers to fit through comfortably. A tape measure, plastic coated and marked on both sides, preferably with one side metric, is a help. Tailor's chalk and a soft 2B pencil for marking fabrics. Steel dressmakers' pins will save marks on fabrics. Medium and heavy duty sewing needles will take care of different weight fabrics. Use a heavy needle with heavy duty thread. Use heavy duty mercerised thread for slipcovers and curtains, and the regular dress-making weight for cotton sheer curtains. Sew synthetics with a fine needle and super sheen thread, and always cut the selvages off before sewing, to prevent puckering. All sewing threads come in a wide range of colours, so matching thread to fabric presents no problem.

Keep an iron and ironing board beside you and press as you sew. Use a long table to cut fabrics and a card table close to your sewing machine will support the heavy weight of slipcovers and long draperies as you work on them.

When you shop for furnishing fabrics, take the exact measurements of the window, sofa, bed or chair with you. Check with the salesman that you have allowed enough for turnings, fullness in the case of sheers, pattern repeats if the fabric is printed. Buy only the type of fabric that is suitable for the job to be done. It pays to buy fabrics that are guaranteed washable, colourfast, and reasonably shrinkproof. A good brand name and a trained fabric salesman are your best guides.

Whenever you can, buy the most economical width of fabric for your purpose. Some sheers are made in widths to 120in which saves seaming if a large window is to be covered. Choose linings that are the same widths as the fabrics for more economical cutting. Do not be afraid to use new fabrics, learn how to handle them.

For nylon or Terylene nets use nylon or Terylene thread and stitch seams over tissue paper, pulling it away later.

For plastic curtains for bathrooms use talcum powder on the machine plate and use a fairly long stitch.

For vinyls use linen or Terylene thread and a large stitch. A mixture of equal parts of glycerine and water rubbed along the seams will prevent your machine sticking to the vinyl.

For fibreglass fabric use a mercerised thread, a long stitch, a loose tension on top-to-bottom threads and very light pressure on the pressure foot.

Pre-shrink all piping cord before making it up, unless guaranteed pre-shrunk.

Before cutting fabric find the true cross-grain of your fabric. Firm plain weaves can be torn. Heavy linens, textured and novelty weaves do not tear easily—pull a thread cross-wise and cut along this line.

Square up all fabrics by pulling from the corners on the bias, press straight with an iron.

How to sew furnishing fabrics

Today furnishing fabrics vary in weight so it is important to use the right needle, the right sewing thread and the right length of stitch. They can be sewn successfully on a home sewing machine, so here is a general guide:

Fabric	Thread	Machine needle size	Stitches per inch
Net, lace, organdie, voile, fine cotton, gingham, lawn.	No 60 cotton or mercerised thread	11-14 depending on weight of fabric	16-14 according to fineness of fabric
Man-made fibres: nylon Terylene, polyesters, sheers, etc.	nylon or Terylene threads	11 (sew over tissue paper and pull away later)	12-15 according to fineness of fabric
Cotton, linen, rayon, chintz, fine cord, velvet, textured cottons, etc.	No 40 cotton or mercerised thread	16	14
Heavy linen, burlap, tweed, brocade, velour, moquette, denim.	No 24 cotton or mercerised thread	18	12-14

To adjust your machine: In your sewing machine manual you will find instructions for adjusting your machine to the right tension, the right pressure on the pressure foot and a balanced stitch. These adjustments vary with different fabrics, so test on scraps of the fabrics before you start.

The wrong tension causes puckered seams and weak stitching. Light tension is needed on synthetics and blended fabrics. Too much pressure on the pressure foot makes the top layer of fabric ripple as you stitch, too little makes such a loose seam that stitches will show when the seam is pressed open.

A well-balanced stitch will look the same on both sides. If you are using mercerised thread test your stitching by folding a square of fabric in half diagonally, make a row of stitching ½in from and parallel to this fold. Grasp the stitching with thumb and forefinger of each hand about 2in apart and pull with a snap to make the threads break. If both threads break you have a balanced stitch and the right tension adjustment. If the top thread only breaks, loosen the upper tension; if only the bottom thread breaks, loosen the bobbin tension.

For good stitching: Keep your machine clean and oiled. It is important to maintain a steady, even pace when stitching, if it is done in spurts your stitching will be uneven. Use a metal thimble for handsewing, find one that fits your middle finger comfortably, firmly and snugly. If it tends to slip off, moisten the end of your finger so suction will help to hold the thimble in place.

Press hems and seams well: The best iron is a combination steam-and-dry. Those irons that give steam at low settings are useful for blends and synthetic fabrics. When working on curtains and other large articles a small table beside your ironing board will help to hold them.

Aids for making home furnishings

Tapes, cords, hooks, tie backs and decorative metal finishes for poles, and rods are readily available from the home furnishing section of department stores.

There are pleater tapes with uniformly spaced pockets for use with four-pronged drapery hooks. The tape is sewn to the top of the curtains. This tape is firm enough to serve as a heading. Insert the hooks to form the pleats. The tape not only saves hours of measuring and stitching in making the curtains, but makes washing and ironing easy, since the hooks are simply pulled out and the curtains laundered as flat pieces of fabric. Tapes are usually 3in and 4in wide.

Buckram, a type of stiff net, is used for headings on curtains and for making pelmets. It may be used instead of pleater tapes when you want to sew pleats down on silk curtains that will be dry cleaned.

Piping cords for use on slipcovers, bedspreads and cushions come in different weights. They need to be covered with a bias cut strip of the fabric being used. They are sewn into the seams to give a professional finish.

Tapes with cords already inserted and slots for curtain rings are also available for making shirred headings on sheer curtains. They are particularly useful in making Roman and Austrian shades. Cords for drawing up blinds are available by the yard.

Weights for curtains and draperies may be bought individually. They are meant to be covered with fabric and sewn to the bottoms of the side seams to make curtains hang well. For lighter fabrics a chain type of weight, sold by the yard, is laid in the bottom hem of the curtain.

Decorative fringes and tapes for trims come in a wide variety of designs, styles, colours and widths.

An elegant dining setting enhanced by a beautiful curtain backdrop.

How to Make Curtains

THE basic shape of windows can be transformed by skilful curtain treatments. Curtains can make small rooms look larger, reduce a ceiling's height or unify a varied-size collection of windows.

Choice of fabric will depend on the amount of shade and privacy needed; on whether the room's decoration scheme is to stem from the curtain pattern or to be a foil for existing furnishings. Some fabrics are better for informal rooms, others lend themselves to tailored effects, still others make a room look bright and airy.

Measuring up

To calculate the basic amount of fabric needed, measure the width of the window (diag 1A). The measurement should cover the width of the glass, plus as much overlap at sides and centre as required.

The total curtain width, whether it is made up of two or more curtains, should be at least one and a half times the total measurement of the window width, plus overlaps.

A repeat design on a patterned fabric must hang at the same level right across the curtains. Before buying your fabric check the length of the repeat and calculate the extra length needed to allow for wastage in matching the pattern.

It is wise to add 1½in a yard to allow for possible shrinkage in fabrics that are not guaranteed pre-shrunk.

Measure the length: (diag 1B) for a sill-length curtain or (diag 1C) for a floor-length curtain.

Add to this length an allowance for the hem and heading tape (allow about double the width of the tape) plus an allowance for the bottom hem; 3in for short curtain, 5in for long.

To calculate the yardage, divide the width of your fabric into the total curtain width to find the number of widths you need, then multiply this number by the overall length of the curtains.

Preparing fabric

Carefully measure each length of fabric for the curtains with a tape measure, allowing for turnings and pattern matching before cutting.

Mark the top of every length to ensure that the fabric runs in the same direction on each curtain.

Be sure to cut the fabric absolutely straight. When joining widths of fabric match the pattern carefully at the join.

Cut selvages off altogether or clip at intervals right through them to prevent any drag.

Finish off raw edges neatly and press all seams.

Use French seams on fabrics tending to fray. On heavier fabrics flat seams with raw edges trimmed with pinking shears will suffice.

If using pull-up tape be sure to leave ends of cord free.

Measure length of curtain, turn up hem and tack. Hang curtains at the windows for a few days before finally adjusting the length and stitching the hem.

Pelmets: These are used to hide the curtain rail when curtains are open. If you plan to have pleated or frilled pelmets at the top of the curtain measure the pelmet or valance rail including the two returns, these are the sections of rail which bend back at each end and join the wall.

For box pleating multiply 2½ times the length of the rail by 12in, this gives a pelmet or valance 8in deep with allowance for turnings. Printed and patterned fabrics need an extra ½yard to allow for pattern repeat. For frilling, allow half the width of the rail again and multiply by 12in.

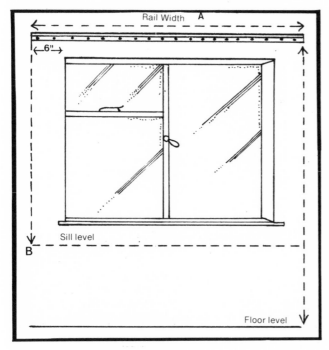

MEASURING WINDOWS

Lining: Linings will prevent your curtains fading in strong sunlight. Having calculated your curtain fabric you will need the same amount of lining fabric, but omit the allowance for pattern matching. Cotton sateen is one of the best fabrics for lining curtains. There is also an insulating material that may be used for lining, this prevents heat entering a room in summer and keeps a room warmer in winter by preventing heat escaping.

Choose lining colours carefully especially if you plan to use the same colour lining on all curtains so that they look uniform from the outside of the house.

Headings
Curtain tops which are left visible can be very elegant.

Special pleating tapes and hooks are available for making gathered or pleated headings. Stitch the tapes with pockets for hooks to the top of the curtain and use the pleater hooks to make the pinch pleats as desired.

More material must be allowed for the curtain width if it is to be pleated. The fabric allowance should be at least twice the width of the track across the window, and an allowance of 4in to 6in should be made for each curtain length for the top hem.

Velvet curtains
Be sure the pile runs in the same direction on each curtain length of fabric. For a silkier look and an easier to brush one that prevents dust collecting, hang the curtains with the pile DOWN.

Line velvet curtains for preference. If unlined, all hems should be handsewn. Never press velvet flat. Steam all hems and turnings carefully by passing the iron lightly across the fabric without pressure.

Net and sheer
Sheer curtains never look attractive when skimped. Allow three times the width of the window when calculating fabric requirements. Make all seams as narrow as possible and turn narrow hems.

Use a fine needle and Terylene thread on man-made fibres.

Use lightweight tapes for the headings. It is more satisfactory to buy a ready-made frilling than to make it yourself.

What you need to know to make curtains

Cutting: Pin Terylene and other flimsy materials to paper when cutting. They are less slippery that way and easier to handle.

Draw cords: These are threaded through heading tapes sewn to the tops of curtains. Draw the cords to gather the curtains.

Facing: A piece of self or different fabric sewn on separately.

Fitment: Pole, wire, rod or runner on which curtains are hung.

Heading: The top hem of the curtain, or the top half of the top hem. Frills, pleats are used.

Heading tape: This tape is sewn to the top of the curtains. It is slotted to take hooks or rings, but can also have draw cords to gather sheer and unlined curtains.

Materials: Never buy curtain material until you know exactly what the material is made of. Velvet originally made from silk can now be nylon, cotton or rayon. It drapes well but needs special care and cleaning. Satin can be silk or rayon which will not wash and should be dry cleaned and cotton satin which can be washed. Nylon mixed with other yarns helps to prevent shrinkage and creasing. Terylene is hard wearing, will wash well and pleat well. Always ask if material is pre-shrunk, washable and fast dye.

Sewing threads: Use cotton thread on cotton fabric, silk on silk, Terylene on Terylene, silk on rayon.

Shrinkage: Net curtains may shrink. It is a good plan to include an extra tuck in top or bottom hem to be picked out after the first washing.

Slot case: This is the lower part of the top hem, divided from it by a line of stitching. The ends are open for the wire or rod.

Stitching: When machining, keep the bulk of your work on the left-hand side. Seam always in the same direction, if possible, so that the fabric is pushed the same way. Trim the selvages of Terylene before sewing seams to prevent drag.

Tension: Test tension before starting curtain by stitching on a scrap of material, on the double bias, and pulling it. If thread snaps tension is too tight. Even a quarter turn of the adjustment screw has a marked effect.

Valance: A separate frill hung from side to side above the curtain.

Valance rail: The rod or runner standing out from the curtain rail to hold pleated or frilled valance.

Wire or rod: Used where the curtains do not have to be drawn to and fro. It is excellent for curtains that remain in position all the time.

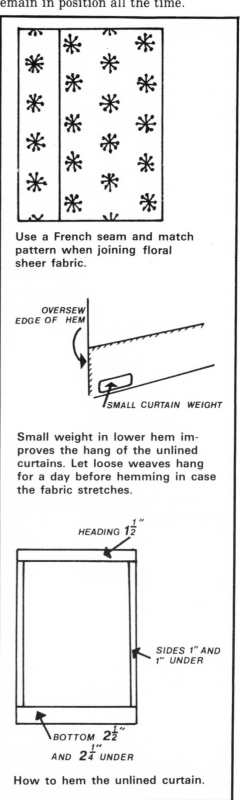

Use a French seam and match pattern when joining floral sheer fabric.

OVERSEW EDGE OF HEM

SMALL CURTAIN WEIGHT

Small weight in lower hem improves the hang of the unlined curtains. Let loose weaves hang for a day before hemming in case the fabric stretches.

HEADING $1\frac{1}{2}''$

SIDES $1''$ AND $1''$ UNDER

BOTTOM $2\frac{1}{2}''$ AND $2\frac{1}{4}''$ UNDER

How to hem the unlined curtain.

CURTAIN MAKING HINTS

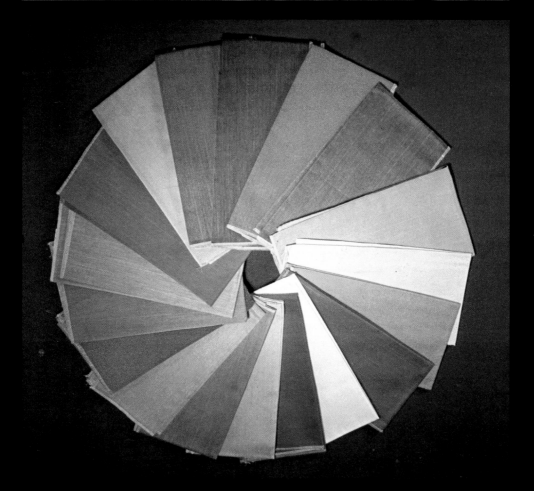

Sometimes curving folds in a curtain will do more to enhance a room than straight ones. With this fabric the patterns and stripes must continue across the width of the curtain.

Do's and Don'ts for curtain making

1. **Do** be bold. Timidity leads to the use of so-called 'safe colours' and this can mean dull decorating.
2. **Do** seek the advice of experts. At good furnishing stores experienced staff are always ready to help.
3. **Do** choose all fabrics in both daylight and artificial light, for only in this way can you gauge the colour.
4. **Do** remember that lined curtains hang better and last longer.
5. **Do** remember that colours on a glossy surface will seem much brighter than those on a matt surface.
6. **Don't** choose curtains from materials spread out on a counter. They should be hung and looked at against the light.
7. **Don't** ruin the effect by skimping. Allow plenty of material for fullness; twice the width of your windows for heavy materials, and three times the width of the windows for sheer materials.
8. **Don't** wash curtains unless you're certain they are safe in water. It is better to have them dry cleaned.
9. **Don't** choose a fabric unless you are sure it will suit your style of room.
10. **Don't** be sidetracked. Make your own choice or be guided by experts.

How to mitre a corner: With right sides together fold corner of square diagonally in half. From raw edges measure depth of hem required and mark on fold with a pin. Fold point over in line with pin; with pencil, lightly mark sloped side of point on to fabric as shown in diagram 1. Stitch on this line. Fasten ends off securely. Trim away point leaving ¼in turning. Turn corner to right side and press in place with seam through middle of corner (diag 2). Continue to make hem in the usual way.

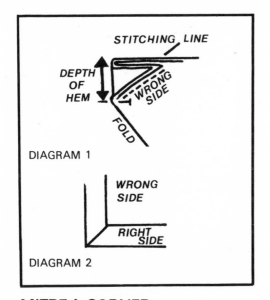

MITRE A CORNER

How to Make Unlined Curtains

Unlined curtains are the easiest of all to make, but like all sewing jobs, must be done correctly to look attractive. These simple instructions will make the job easy for you.

Here is how you estimate how much fabric you will need for a simple pair of draped curtains:

First measure the width of your window. This is the width of fabric you will need for one curtain. Where necessary sew two or more widths together for each curtain.

To work out the length of each unsewn curtain, measure the distance from curtain rail to the point you want the curtains to finish.

Add up to 12in for hems and shrinkage (that is, if the material has not been pre-shrunk). If the fabric has a large pattern repeat, add the length of one complete pattern to ensure accurate matching of each curtain pattern.

You may find you need to add a half-width of fabric to each curtain for fullness. If so, cut the length of 48in-wide fabric down the centre and join the selvage edge of each 24in-wide piece to the selvage edge of each curtain. Narrowly hem the cut edge of each curtain. You can, of course, join whole 48-in widths.

To hem: Make narrow side hems (about ½in), make a 3in hem along bottom. If you have allowed extra fabric for shrinking, include this amount in the bottom hem, leaving the hem tacked until the curtains are first washed. Adjust then, if necessary.

To pleat: Pleating curtains without using tape is difficult. Buy ready-made pleating tape for an easy job. Lay the ready-made pleating tape on top of the lining and curtain heading (slot openings to the bottom), and stitch to curtain by machining along both long edges.

Insert the special pleating hooks in the slots at the required intervals and attach to the curtain rail runners.

Last step is to finish the top of the curtains. To do this measure from bottom hem up each side edge and mark the required length of curtain with a pin on each side. From pin to pin fold top of curtains down on wrong side and trim this turning to depth of heading required—say 1in to 1½in. Cut a length of curtain tape 1in longer than the width of curtains.

Turn under each cut end of tape for ½in and tack.

If the tape is fitted with cords which are later drawn up to drape the curtain, pull these free before turning under the ends of tape.

Place the tape across the top of the curtain on the wrong side, with its top edge well below the top fold of curtain, and its lower edge covering the raw edge of hem.

Sew top and bottom edges of tape to curtain. (Loosely knot cords at one end of the tape and leave them free at the other end.) See diagram below.

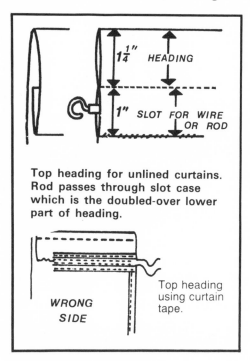

Top heading for unlined curtains. Rod passes through slot case which is the doubled-over lower part of heading.

WRONG SIDE

Top heading using curtain tape.

UNLINED CURTAINS

How to Make Lined Curtains

Despite their elegant look, lined draperies are not difficult to make. The lining protects the more delicate drapery fabrics from soiling and fading and also gives a uniform outside appearance to windows. Before you buy your material, measure up accurately; this will save you a lot of time and money later.

To measure the length of material required, run your tape from the curtain rail or ring to within one inch of the window ledge, or, for a longer curtain that will help to exclude the draught, 6in below the window ledge, or within 1in of the floor. Add 5in if the heading is to be simply gathered; 9in if it is to be deep or pleated.

If you choose a patterned material, you may need to allow extra yardage so that the pattern matches on each length. You can only calculate the amount when you have selected the pattern and know the length of each repeat. Lining should be 2in shorter

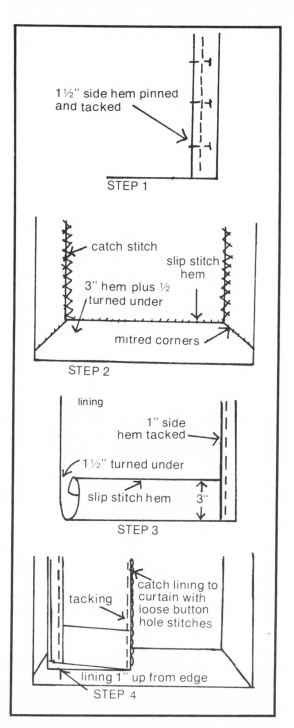

1½" side hem pinned and tacked

STEP 1

catch stitch

slip stitch hem

3" hem plus ½ turned under

mitred corners

STEP 2

lining

1" side hem tacked

1½" turned under

slip stitch hem

3"

STEP 3

tacking

catch lining to curtain with loose button hole stitches

lining 1" up from edge

STEP 4

LINED CURTAINS

than the curtain length and 1in narrower than the width.

When calculating the width, allow one and a half times the length of the curtain rail; or twice the length of the rail if it is very long, when you will need to join the material. If you decide to have double or triple pleats along the heading, you will need to join the material.

Allow an extra 6in wherever curtains are to overlap.

A good overlap helps to exclude draughts. Allow 1½in for side turnings, or ½in for any side that is to be joined to another. Almost the same yardage is needed for the lining, minus the amount allowed for matching pattern.

Here are simple, straightforward instructions for making lined curtains:

Step 1: If more than one width of material is used in a curtain, join by machining together with matching thread.

Turn in 1½in side hems, pin and tack. Do not cut off selvage unless it is very tight. Sew both sides, working from left to right with a catch stitch.

Step 2: Turn up hem 3in and allow ½in to turn under. Pin, tack. Mitre corners as shown in diagram; do not cut any fabric away if you are using velvet or other heavy material. (Note that each mitred corner starts a little way up the side.) Slipstitch hem and along mitred corners, being careful thread does not show on right side.

Step 3: Cut lining the same size as the curtain, plus 3½in longer for hem. Turn hem of lining up 4½in—that is, a 1½in fold under a 3in hem. Pin, tack, slipstitch hem. Turn side hems in 1in and tack. Do not stitch yet.

Step 4: Fold lining in half, lengthwise, and place on half of curtain. Make certain it is even. Tack down centre fold to hold lining in place. Catch lining to curtain with small buttonhole stitches along tacking line. Leave thread quite loose, as diagram. Take out tacking. Repeat every 12 to 15in, according to the width of the curtain.

Step 5: Tack and slipstitch lining to curtain at sides. Slipstitch hem of lining to curtain, for 2in only, along each side.

Step 6: Measure required length of curtain from bottom hem. If a pelmet is to be added, the allowance for the heading above the tape when finished is about 1in, therefore, allow 3in for heading—1½in when turned down.

If no pelmet is to be used, you will need a deeper heading. Allow 5in—2½in when turned down. Turn down heading, smoothing out lining underneath, tack and slipstitch. Gather curtain with two rows of gathers, using strong thread. If very large, gather in sections. Draw up to required size, usually about half curtain measurement.

Step 7: You will need heading tape, 1½in wide,

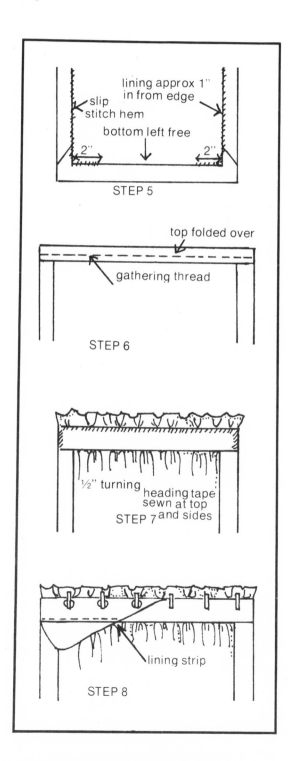

STEP 5

STEP 6

STEP 7

STEP 8

usually half curtain width, plus ½in for each side for turnings. Sew each side, then pin tape into position. Equalise gathers on curtain, tack tape and sew top securely to curtain.

Step 8: Cut a strip of lining the size of the heading tape, plus good turnings. Tack to underneath of tape (which has not yet been sewn down). Secure lining and heading tape to curtain at this edge. Sew hooks to tape, first one each end, then others every 2 to 2½in. Sew lining to tape.

Net Curtains (Classic Style)

NET curtains are quick and easy to make.

Step 1: Cut to required length, plus turnings. Allow good turnings: bottom hem, 5in (2½in and 2½in turned under); heading with slot case, 4½in.

Step 2: If more than one width of fabric is to be used in one curtain, join with small French seam. Cut off selvage.

Step 3: Cut selvage off sides. Turn in 1in and 1in under. Pin, tack. Slipstitch hem if sewing by hand, or machine with fine thread same colour as net. Press with warm iron. Care must be taken with Terylene that iron is not too hot.

Step 4: For bottom hem, average curtain, make 2½in hem with 2½in turned under. Pin, tack, slipstitch with fine, matching thread. Use deeper hems for longer curtains.

Step 5: Top heading. Measure required length of curtain from finished bottom hem. Add 4½in for heading and slot case. If a wide rod is to be used, allow extra. Slipstitch hem or machine; stitch between heading and slot case to divide them. If curtain is very long and is to be drawn to and fro, sew gathering tape to take hooks for runners, in place of wire slot.

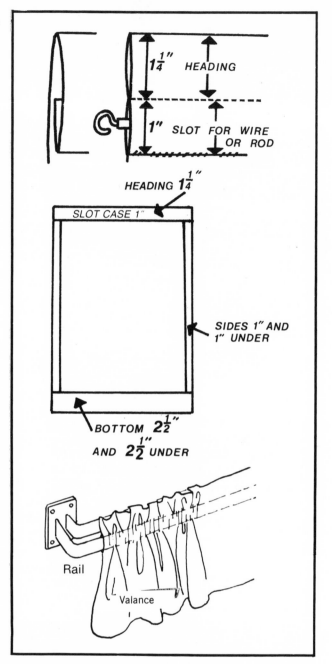

NET CURTAINS

Sheer curtains with lined side drapes.

Unlined pinch pleated curtains.

Draped Cross-over Curtains

DRAPED cross-over curtains are usually made up in pairs so that two curtains overlap at the top with a single heading and the same rod. The overlap may be a small one in the centre of the window or the complete width of the pane according to your sizes and how much of the glass you want to cover.

Find the necessary length of material by measuring from the top left-hand corner of the window in a loose curve to the bottom right-hand corner A-D. Add 12in for the tail, plus 6in to 8in for hems and shrinkage. This is your maximum length.

Multiply this total by two for a pair of curtains. In width you need two to two and a half times the window's width for cotton or nylon net and up to three times the width for fine sheers.

Cut the curtains to the maximum length, checking that the grain is straight.

As the tail must be cut on an angle measure the height of the window frame from C-D and add the allowance for tail and hems. This will be your minimum length and the curtains will end at the sill.

Mark this measurement on the outside (right) edge of the right-hand curtain, and on the left edge of the opposite curtain. Draw a line with chalk linking the maximum hem with the minimum hem and check carefully before you cut your fabric. There can be a difference from 9in upwards. Turn over a small rolled hem along the slanting edge. This may be finished with frilling or a shell edge.

To hang the curtains in pairs, keep the slanting edge to the bottom. Lay one curtain over the other, right sides downwards. If the width of the double thickness of curtain is about twice the total width of the window frame you can have a complete cross-over with the necessary fullness. If it is the same width or less, move the top curtain sideways until the width measures from 2 to 2½ times the window size. This will reduce the actual overlap in the centre, but for a wide window it gives a very good effect.

Pin the curtains together along the top, turn down a heading hem of about 1½in and stitch on the curtain tape over the raw edge. Or if you are hanging the curtains on a light rod or plastic coated wire, use a plain tape to form a casing.

Gather up the curtain cord or thread the rod through the top until curtain width is the same as window frame size. Your curtains will hang in soft folds. Loop back the ends at the lower corners of the window with plain ties made from scraps of curtain fabric and fixed to a wall hook.

With a very wide window where a complete cross-over is not necessary, calculate your maximum length of curtain by measuring from B to D, but allow the same looping curve for the drapery.

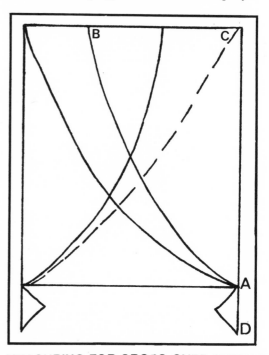

MEASURING FOR CROSS-OVER CURTAINS

Another way to make draped cross-over curtains

The width of each curtain should be about twice the width of the window. Measure the required length of curtain at side from top of window (C-D) add extra length for turnings and heading. It is usual to have frilling at the draped side and the bottom of the curtain.

Frilling by the yard can be bought ready to sew on the curtain. If you make your own, cut enough 6in wide strips from the width of the material to equal twice the long side and the bottom of the curtain. Seam the strips together and hem all around the edges of the resulting long strip.

Use the gathering attachment on the sewing machine to gather the strip, reducing it to half its length. Place stitching 1in in from long edge of the strip.

To make: Measure off one required length of curtain, plus turning allowance. Lay fabric flat on floor, mark off the window length on one side of the material and from this point cut off the bottom diagonally to the opposite corner. Trim off the selvages and make a small double hem along the sides and bottom of the curtain.

Machine the frill to the longer side and bottom edge of the curtain, placing the stitching on top of the gathering stitches. Lay the frill over the wrong side of the hem to do this, so that the side of the curtain that faces the window will have a finished appearance.

Make up another curtain in the reverse way. Lay one curtain flat on the floor and place the other curtain two-thirds of the way over it so that the longer edges are overlapping. Pin the curtains together at the top, then tack. Turn down top hem and sew through both curtains to make a slot for the curtain rod or wire.

Curtain bands of the same material will hold the drapes in place. To make bands cut a 6in wide strip of fabric by the required length. Fold in half widthwise and add frill on one side as you stitch together. Sew curtain rings to the ends of each strip. These can be slipped over a hook screwed into the windowframe.

Cafe Curtains

CAFE curtains are a popular choice for the modern home. Short enough to give a view, they can have very distinctive decorations and trimmings.

When planning your cafe curtains, first put up the rods. It is easy to make a mistake in measuring if you haven't placed the rods in position.

Width of curtains should be at least twice the width of the window. Length of curtains should be measured from the top of rod to wherever you want the bottom of curtain to end. Then add 9½in to this measurement for top, tab turn-over and the hem.

To make a basic cafe curtain:

Step 1: Cut each panel to required length. If using print, cut all panels to match. (Allow extra yardage for matching.)

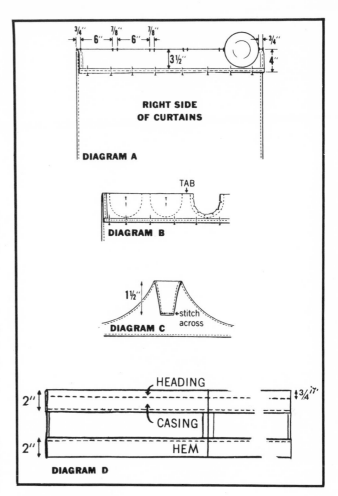

CAFE CURTAINS

Step 2: On side edges, turn selvages under ½in, stitch.

Step 3: Turn top edge under ½in, stitch.

Step 4: Fold top edge 4in to right side. Pin as shown. Press.

Step 5: To mark scallops, use a 6in saucer. (Be sure saucer measures exactly 6in across centre.) Along top fold of curtain, mark intervals as shown in Diagram A which illustrates a panel finished to a 35in width.

Step 6: Place saucer in 6in intervals, with bottom edge at raw edge of hem, as shown. (Use raw edge of hem as guide for saucer.) Mark out scallops with pencil.

Step 7: Pin the two thicknesses together through centre of scallops. Stitch around scallops. Trim out scallops ¼in from stitching. Notch seam allowance as shown (diag B).

Step 8: Turn to right side, bringing out corners of tabs between scallops; press. Topstitch along edge of scallops.

Step 9: Fold each tab 1½in to wrong side, forming a loop. Stitch across end of tab as shown (diag C), making sure to reverse stitching at each end of stitching line to secure thread.

Step 10: Turn raw edge ½in to wrong side; turn-up and stitch 3in hem. Press. Your basic curtain is now finished and ready to trim, or hang as it is.

An important finishing touch—the thing that often gives that professional look—is the valance (diag D).

A valance is generally cut to 17in (for a 12in finished height) and to two times the width of the window. Cut as many 17in wide strips across the fabric as you need for the desired width. Sew strips together along the selvage edge. Make narrow hems on ends and 2in hems at top and bottom edges. Run a row of stitching ¾in in from top edge of top hem to make heading and casing.

If you prefer to use a simple heading at the top of the curtain, instead of the scallops, measure from top of rod to window sill or where you want bottom of curtain to be. Add only 7in to length you want your finished curtain to be—3½in for top hem, heading and casing, and 3½in for bottom hem. Follow directions for top of valance.

Festoon Curtains

FESTOON curtains are a practical way of covering a window that opens on a dull view, a bay window or a door where they remain stationary.

They should be made from a washable fabric that needs no ironing, since they are almost impossible to iron satisfactorily. Fine fabrics such as nylon, nets and fine muslins are most suitable for making this type of curtain as they will hang softly and look attractive all the time. They are easy to make if you use a special gathering tape with draw cords so that the fabric can be gathered evenly and the curtains will hang well. They do need quite a lot of fabric. Allow at least 1½ times the width of the window and twice to three times the length of the window. The number of ruches or festoons will depend on the width of the window, three for a small one to seven or nine for a very wide one will make your curtain look in proportion with the window size. Allow 9in to 10in between each ruching.

To make: Start by making your curtain in the ordinary way, a 2½in hem down each side, a 4in hem at the bottom and a 3in hem at the top. On the wrong side sew the tape with the cords verti-cally down the sides of the curtain, starting 3in from the bottom. At equal distances across the curtain sew the tapes vertically the length of the curtain. All tapes must be perfectly matched, their slots in line across the curtain. This is most important, for your curtain will only hang evenly if this part is carefully done.

Starting from the bottom insert ⅝in split curtain rings in every fourth slot.

Draw the vertical cords up to the size of the window and knot securely.

So that the fabric ruches will hang evenly across the curtain handsew the gathers to the tape every four inches or so to hold them.

Small hooks on the window frame linked to small rings on the side of the curtain will hold the curtain in position on a door that opens and shuts.

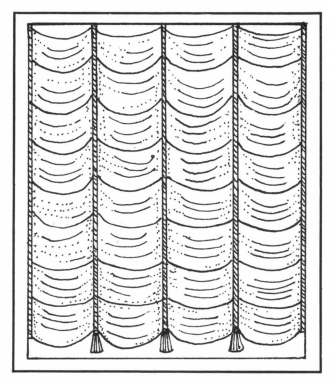

FESTOON CURTAINS

There are many variations of cafe curtains.

Lined curtains give an elegant background to a dining area.

Bathroom Curtains

BATHROOM window curtains can be made from any type of fabric, waterproof or not, if the window is far enough away from the shower so that the curtain will not get wet. Use plastic if window is near the shower. These can be cut and sewn like ordinary fabric, using a large needle and long stitches.

For shower curtains you can use any material you like. Plastic and terry towelling make practical curtains, other fabrics may need to have a protective lining.

Lining may be attached directly to the shower curtains with snap fasteners to ensure easy removal for laundering. Give individuality to your bathroom by adding pleats to your curtains, both at the windows and the shower recess. Decorative braids and fringes give an extra fillip to the bathroom when sewn to the sides and bottom of the curtains. Braids can also make attractive tie-backs for the different curtains in the bathroom.

Scalloped headings outlined with fringe add a distinctive note. Repeat this trimming in spaced rows down the curtains for added interest, especially if your curtains are in solid colours.

Use curtains as the basis of your colour scheme. Match or contrast towels with them. Pick up the colours of printed curtains with your towels—and soap. The bathroom usually needs a lot of imagination to give it individuality.

Curtains to Cover Air Conditioners

AIR CONDITIONERS are a boon in warm weather. Most are installed in windows and this makes successful curtaining of the window quite a problem. One would like to enjoy the comfort of an air-conditioned room without the unsightly look of a protruding air conditioner.

Here are four suggestions to make the air conditioner less conspicuous, while at the same time, the window treatment adds to the decor of the room.

Austrian or festoon curtains are easy to make—you will find directions on page 98.

Cafe curtains in tiers and hung on rods are easy to draw back and forth over the window. See page 97 for directions.

Cross-over tie-back curtains in sheer fabric will give light from the top part of the window, and at the same time, conceal the air conditioner.

A top curtain or deep valance, plus a curtain that reaches the floor and hung on a brass rod will give a dressed-up look. They are simple in style and take little time to make and hang.

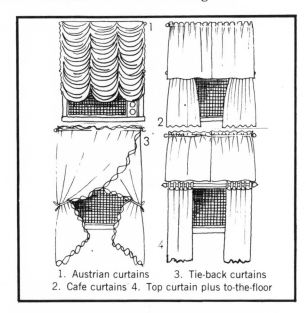

1. Austrian curtains   3. Tie-back curtains
2. Cafe curtains 4. Top curtain plus to-the-floor

CURTAINS TO COVER AIR CONDITIONERS

Style at the Top

The most important part of curtain style is the top of the curtain and this is where there is scope for originality. The choice is wide: gathered or pleated valances, formal pelmets, decorative headings and graceful swags.

Valances

Gathered or pleated valances can be most attractive. A valance is, in fact, a very short curtain, and should be made up in the same way as an unlined curtain. Fabric should be estimated in the same way as for the curtain. Always cut from selvage to selvage, never with selvages along top and bottom edge.

Valances may be from 4in to 12in deep, though 8in is average. Valance headings can be gathered or pleated in the same way as curtains.

The valance can be attached to a separate valance rail with curtain tape, or it can be hung by an expanded wire slipped through a channel made in the valance below the heading.

Pelmets

Most curtains need a pelmet to give them a finished appearance and, as a general rule, the pelmet should be roughly one-eighth the curtain depth.

How to make your own pelmets:
The following materials will be needed: upholstery buckram for stiffening and making shape; fabric to match curtains; lining; braid or fringe for finishing.

Step 1: Measure front and sides of curtains. Make a paper pattern to the size and shape required. Try your pattern against the window.

Step 2: Place paper pattern on buckram and mark around with tailor's chalk. Cut out on the chalk line.

Step 3: Place paper pattern on wrong side of material and pin. Allow 1½in turning all round. If material is printed or figured, placement of pattern must be considered. Cut material to shape, including the turnings.

Step 4: Place material right side downwards on the table, making sure that there are no creases. Lay the buckram shape on this. Fold the edges of the material over the buckram, first pinning and then tacking with long, loose stitches. Press with a warm iron; the fabric should stick to the buckram.

Step 5: With the right side of the pelmet facing, place the braid or the fringe in place and tack with long, loose stitches. Sew through to the buckram.

Step 6: To line the pelmet, cut lining 1in larger all round than the buckram, to allow for turnings. Fold top edge of lining down 1in and place on top of the pelmet. Pin, then tack. Fold all the lining in the same way. Slipstitch the lining to the material.

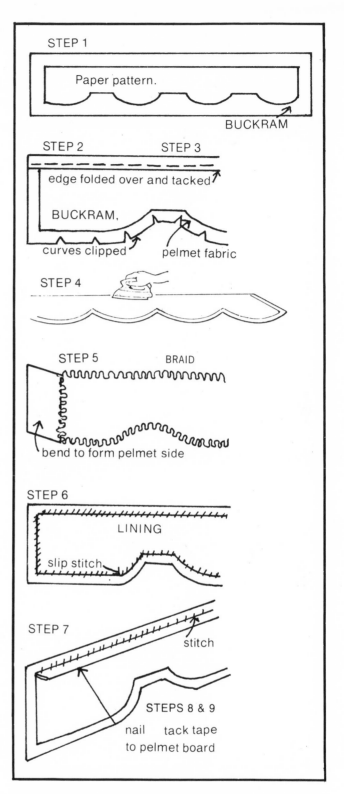

STEP 1

Paper pattern.

BUCKRAM

STEP 2   STEP 3

edge folded over and tacked

BUCKRAM,

curves clipped   pelmet fabric

STEP 4

STEP 5   BRAID

bend to form pelmet side

STEP 6

LINING

slip stitch

STEP 7

stitch

STEPS 8 & 9

nail   tack tape

to pelmet board

Step 7: Take a piece of 1½in wide heading tape the width of the pelmet plus ¾in turnings at each end. Fold tape in half and tack to the upper edge of the pelmet.

Step 8: Pin the folded heading tape to the back of the pelmet. Stitch its top edge firmly through to the lining and buckram, lower edge free.

Step 9: Tack or nail the free edge of the tape to the cornice or pelmet board.

101

Decorative Curtain Headings

It is very easy to create a special effect with your curtains. Here are various types of headings that will give them both a pleasing finish and an interesting drape.

Shirred heading
This can be most easily achieved with shirring tape. Stitch the first row 1in from the top of the curtain, skip an inch and apply another row. Continue until the heading is the desired depth.

Pull the cords for fullness and tie. Release for laundry purposes.

Insert hooks through the tape for hanging. For sheer materials use an elasticised shirring tape—stretch it while stitching it to your material. You will find this to be the easiest way of shirring filmy materials which are often very difficult to handle. When the tape is sewn on, put a split ring through each corner, and hang curtain from the cup hooks.

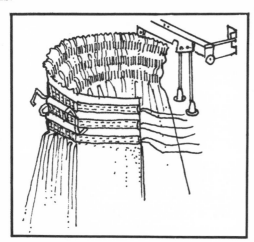

SHIRRED HEADING

Pinch pleats
These make an attractive drapery heading which is one of the most popular in use today. There are usually three groups of pinch pleats to a width of 48in. Allow about three inches for each group and mark position with a pin. Turn down the top edge for 3in, fold pleat as in diagram and tack, stitching with small running stitches. Dotted line of stitching in diagram is 3in and pleat is 3in wide. Divide into three and stitch to form three pleats.

Repeat for the number of pleats needed. Sew heading tape in position, but do not gather. Insert hooks at intervals across the curtain at the back of each pleat.

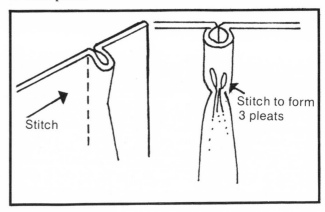

Stitch

Stitch to form 3 pleats

PINCH PLEATS

Box-pleated heading
Measure the space the curtain is to cover plus the rod returns. Width of hemmed fabric minus these two measurements is used for pleats. If result is 25in and you wish five box pleats, allow 5in for each pleat. Stitch stiffening for the heading to wrong side of material, fold over and hem down.

Start first pleat 2in from hemmed edge; mark exact position and width of pleats before stitching. Fold and stitch pleat straight down to 1in below heading. Press flat, tack top and bottom then stitch across the bottom of the pleat.

Box pleats are very decorative when used on the heavier types of materials, such as velvets and brocades for they hang well.

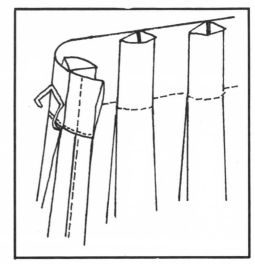

BOX-PLEATED HEADINGS

Cartridge Pleats
These are suitable whenever a particularly formal heading is required. Stitch non-woven interlining

or other stiffening to the wrong side. Determine the space drapery is to cover, plus the rod returns. Width of hemmed fabric, minus these figures is for pleats.

Position pleats carefully, about 2½in each, then carefully stitch down to 1in below the heading. Stuff pleats with paper, cotton, or rolled buckram for a rounded look.

Insert hooks at the back of the pleats and hang the curtains from rods or from ceiling tracks. Cardboard mailing tubes make a wonderful padding for the cartridge pleats and are simple and easy to insert.

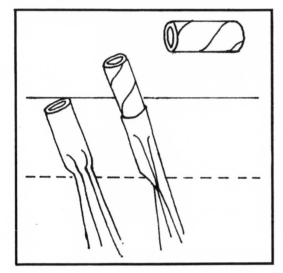

CARTRIDGE PLEATS

Scalloped heading
This is decorative on cafe curtains or curtains that are tied back and require very little fabric.

Divide the width of the curtain equally into the size scallops you require. Make a paper pattern, then mark the curves on material.

Place a facing of the same material as the curtain on it right sides together. Pin, tack, then machine round the curves. Cut them to make a good shape when turned. Press and turn facing out on wrong

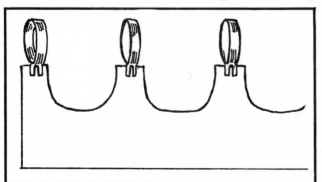

SCALLOPED HEADING

side of curtain. Slipstitch hem facing on to the curtain with small stitches.

Sew rings on curtain at the top of each peak and slip rings over rod.

Window Swags

Many young people today are buying old homes, furnishing them traditionally, and seeking fresh treatment for windows framed in tired convention.

Swags, with their dramatic drapes, meet this need. They are not fussy and are beautiful in simplicity. With a minimum of fabric and trimming they can give the most ordinary window style and importance.

The finished swag and cascades, or jabots, are tacked to an inch-thick board about 4in deep, then attached to the window frame with angle irons.

Tack the swag securely to the board. It can be removed for cleaning.

Swags can be made to match draperies, to pick up one or more of the dominant colours in the room, or to form an eye-catching contrast with curtains and colour scheme. Edge with attractive trimming to emphasise the graceful line.

To make a swag:

Step 1: Lay fabric right side upward on the floor. Mark the centre top of the fabric. Mark the desired width of the swag at the top (A to A diag 1) and the bottom (C to C). Decide the depth of the finished swag. The measurement C to B will vary with the depth of the swag.

Using fabric 36in wide for a 15in deep swag, it will be 4in; 16 in deep will be 5in; 17in deep will be 6in; 18in deep will be 7in; 19in deep will be 8in, and so on. Draw diagonal line from A to B. For five folds divide that diagonal line into sixths. For six folds, into sevenths. For seven folds, into eighths, and so on.

Step 2: Pin the swag at A and A to the side of a bed or settee so that it hangs down. Then pin 1 to A on each side, smoothing in the fold from centre to sides. Then pin 2 to A on each side, and continue until all the folds are pinned in place at A and A on each side.

Step 3: Cut off excess fabric from A on both sides

Pelmets should blend in style and fabric with the curtains and with the room decor.

Curtains with a simple pleated heading.

straight down toward floor. Trim excess along curved bottom of swag, leaving about 3in of fabric after the last fold. Make ½in hem at the top. Sew sides to hold folds in place. Add fringe trim.

Step 4: The cascade or jabots. Measure the length desired for your window. The average is about 30in. Make the width at the top about two-thirds of this measurement, or 20in. Allow 5in for side returns. Either line the cascade, or make ¼in hems. To line, stitch wrong sides of lining and fabric together on three long sides. Turn right side out and press. Overstitch open end. Add fringe trimming.

Step 5: Fold three pleats into cascade or jabot (diag 4). Fold first pleat 4in from long edge to allow for side return. Fold over two remaining pleats, one on top of the other, or slightly spaced. Bind top edge with matching fabric to hold pleats in place. For the other cascade or jabot draw reverse diagonal.

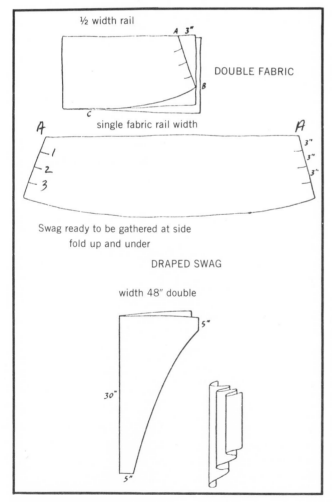

WINDOW SWAGS

Pinch Pleats

Special tapes and hooks are readily available to save all the hard work in making attractive pinch pleats; the hooks may be removed for laundering the curtains and are easier to handle as one long strip of fabric.

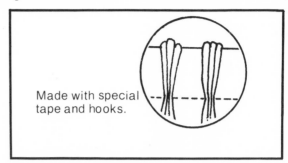

Made with special tape and hooks.

How to make the pinch pleats:
Turn down fabric, and lining if you have used one, ¾in on the wrong side. Place the pleater tape on this hem so that the pockets are equidistant from either end with ½in extra tape at ends for turning under. Stitch pleater tape ¼in from the top, then along the bottom of the tape and at the sides.

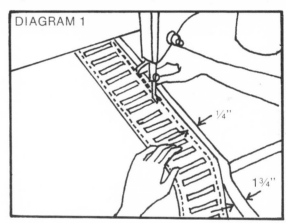

DIAGRAM 1

Insert end hooks in the end pockets. Skip one pocket and insert a pleater hook in the next four pockets of the tape. Insert it carefully so that the pockets remain straight and visible. By checking

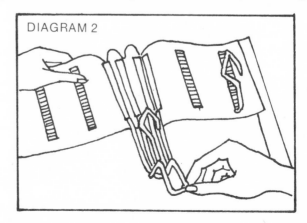

DIAGRAM 2

the front of the pleat you can see if all folds of the pleats are uniform. A little practice and the hooks will go in easily and quickly.

When the hook is in place press the special lock attachment up and in to clip the pleat in position. The pleat will be held firmly from bottom to top. Skip a space and insert another hook in the following four pockets. Continue across the full width of the curtain, until the top is pleated, ending with an end hook.

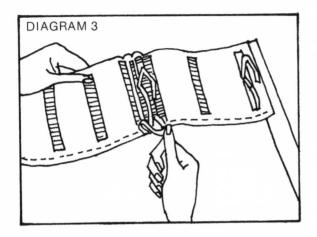

DIAGRAM 3

Hang curtains from the hooks on the pleater hooks by attaching them to the rings on the rollers on the curtain tracks.

To launder curtains, simply release the hooks and pull out of the pockets. The curtain is laundered as one long strip of fabric. After laundering and pressing, rehang curtains by inserting the hooks in the pockets as before.

Interesting Curtain Tops

Diamond-point heading
Cut triangular shaped template from strong cardboard. Use this to cut out the top of your curtain in pointed shapes. Cut interlining to the same shape, and sew to the top of the curtain. Sew small brass rings to each point and hang curtain on a brass rod.

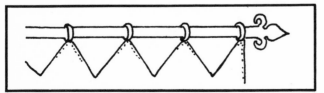

Fringe on top
Put a fringe on top to give new interest to headings of pelmetless curtains. Use a saucer to shape the top of your curtain. Add stiffening. Sheer curtains could be trimmed with permanently pleated nylon— the kind used for lingerie. On plain curtains use a frill of permanently pleated matching cotton.

You can buy several yards of the newest bobble fringes and sew row upon row of them along the top of the curtains for a new and different look. If using long fringe, then one row should be enough, but if you are using narrow fringe, make an impression by sewing on several rows.

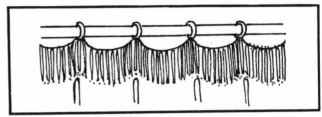

Threaded ribbon
For a window with an inner curtaining of sheer white nylon or Terylene, add colour by suspending it on a brilliant threaded ribbon slotted through brass eyelet holes, and over a brass pole. Use this idea for stationary curtains only, as the ribbon cannot be drawn back.

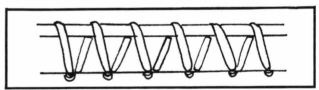

Tab-top curtains
Sew tabs to the tops of your curtains and loop them over a brass rod. This is only suitable for curtains that are permanently in position—not for curtains that are drawn to and fro.

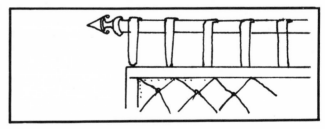

Another idea: sew huge rings to curtain tops and put on a fat pole. A white curtain with multicoloured painted wooden rings would be smart, or a wooden pole painted in a contrast colour or covered with patterned fabric for plain curtains.

Let your imagination run riot. A whole host of exciting ideas can be put into play for interesting and individual curtain tops. There are lots of ways you can introduce colour into your window decor cleverly and simply.

Seeing a 'new chair' take shape is fun and making covers such as on this club chair can give you much satisfaction.

Medieval scallops

Make pattern to the shape desired and place on material. Cut material and stiffening to shape. Sew curtain top. Sew rings to top of each scallop. Hang on rods.

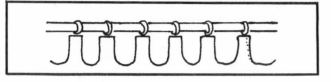

Pinch pleated

A distinctive way to finish off a curtain heading and equally effective for plain or patterned fabrics. Add a glamour touch with fancy pins—say a huge gilt star with a pin at the back—pinned over the bunches of pleats. Slip them out for easy washing.

Button down tabs

Use a cup to shape the scallops between the tabs at the top of your curtain. Allow extra length in the tabs to turn over. Cut stiffening to same shape and sew to curtain top. Turn loops over and secure with a contrast button sewn through loop and curtain. Hang on brass rail.

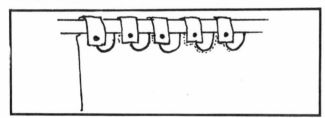

Window Blind

Window blind

A roller blind is quite simple to make. Blind-making kits, containing wooden rollers and bonding fabric, are available in a variety of sizes to fit most windows, if none of these fits your window exactly, buy the nearest size above your window size and cut the roller to fit.

The roller has a rectangular pin and spring fitting at one end which goes at the left of the window. The other end of the roller is bare wood so that you can trim it to the required length if needed. A metal cap and round pin are supplied separately for fitting to the end of the roller.

Choose a fade-resistant, lightweight, closely woven fabric for the blind. Cotton and chintz are excellent, as they hold their shape. On standard fittings rollers turn inwards towards the room so that the wrong side of the rolled up blind will show. To hide the roller fit a pelmet of buckram and fabric to match above the blind.

Also included in the blind-making kit is a length of wood to weight the base of the blind and two metal brackets for hanging the blind. One is slotted to take the rectangular pin at the left of the window, the other has a hole to take the round pin at the right-hand edge.

Fix the roller brackets first, projecting forward from the window frame. Measure from the sill to make sure both brackets are parallel, then measure between them and cut the roller to size if necessary.

To make the blind: It is easiest to make a blind from fabric that is wider than the window, this means there will be no bulky seams. If you do use a narrower fabric then join the widths one on either side of the centre strip, match the patterns carefully and seam them together. Press the seam open and stick the turnings to the wrong side of the fabric to make a smooth seam.

You will need enough fabric to cover the window, plus 5in at the top to cover the roller when the blind is down and 2in at the bottom to make a hem to take the lath. You need the same amount of bonding interlining for stiffening, fabric adhesive for sticking the side hems and fringe or braid for trimming if desired.

Cut your fabric to length and the exact width of the roller. Turn in and press ½in along each side edge. This is to ensure that fabric will clear the fittings if blind rolls up unevenly. Stick the turnings down to the wrong side to make non-bulky hems. Iron-on hemming tape is best. Iron the bonding to the back of the fabric using a hot, dry iron. Press thoroughly to prevent it becoming unstuck, this can take up to one hour of firm pressing. Turn in the side edges of the bonding to meet the fabric hems and slipstitch in place. For a simple straight-edged hem turn and press fabric to wrong side for ½in then make hem about 1½in deep. Machine a second row of stitching close to hem edge. Insert lath in this slot. Hem may be trimmed with fringe, or braid; stab stitch it to the right side of the blind.

An attractive touch of colour added with fringing.

To attach fabric to roller, cut fabric straight across the top. Pass fabric behind the roller with right side in and lining on the outside. Lay the edge against the guideline already marked on the roller and fix to the roller with the tacks provided, setting them about 1in apart.

Note: Always iron the bonding fabric on to the curtain fabric with a dry, hot iron. This releases the adhesive impregnated in the fabric.

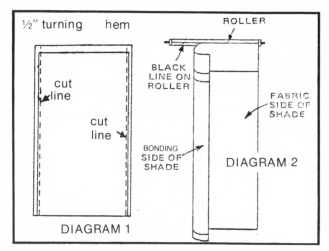

A gay window blind to flatter any room.

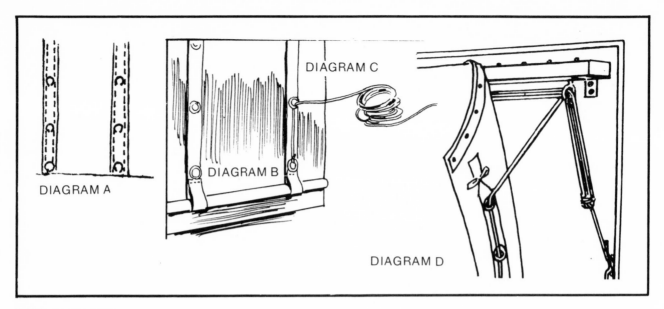

DIAGRAM C

DIAGRAM B

DIAGRAM A

DIAGRAM D

ROMAN SHADE

Window Shade

A Roman shade is an inexpensive, easy-to-make, decorative window treatment. It needs only flat widths of fabric of firm weave. Shirring tape is sewn to the back of the curtain, small rings are inserted in the tape and a cord threaded through the rings to raise or lower the shade.

To make: Cut fabric the width and length of the window to be covered, plus 3in for side hems. Make 1½in side hems. Stitch tape vertically at sides of shade then at intervals (about 12in apart) lengthwise across shade. All tapes must be perfectly matched, their slots exactly in line across the blind. Allow an extra 2in of tape at bottom to hold covered rod. Insert small plastic rings in the tape at regular intervals. Be sure the rings on tapes are even, horizontally (diag A).

Cut a small round brass rod the width of the shade. Cover with fabric and use the extra 2in of tape at the bottom to attach rod to shade. The rod will give the shade the necessary weight to hang firmly (diag B).

Tie lengths of cord to the bottom rings of each tape. Thread cord through rings to the top of the shade (diag C).

Fix top of shade to flat board the width of shade. Attach screw eyes underneath board for traverse cords to go through. Attach cords until shade rises and lowers evenly (diag D).

A decorative tape may be sewn on the right side of plain fabrics to hide the machine stitching used on ring tapes. This gives an added decorative effect to the shade.

For the economy conscious home decorator a Roman shade is inexpensive and simple to make.

Slipcovers

NEW SLIPCOVERS are a substantial economy in home decoration and bring fresh vigour into the colour scheme of your room. Add pattern or texture for interest. Large patterns are more successful than small ones, as the bold design makes a natural centrepiece for the back of the chair. But the larger the pattern repeat, the higher is the amount of wastage. Always measure the chair or settee in detail before buying the material.

It seems a big thing to make your own loose covers, but it is not as complicated as it appears, especially if you start by covering a very simple piece of furniture, progressing to a sofa, only by degrees.

In making a slipcover for a particular piece of furniture, follow exactly the way the upholstery was done and you'll be all right. Cut the fabric for the arms according to the way the upholstery was cut and insert piping in the same places as it is on the upholstery.

Choose the material for slipcovers carefully. It must be tough, hard wearing, firm weave, colourfast and shrink-proof. Beware of a material that is too heavy, bulky rayons and the like. They are difficult to clean and very heavy to handle when sewing them together. Choose a fabric that is suitable for your purpose; one is often tempted to use upholstery woollens, velvets and folk weaves that may shrink badly and be unusable after the first washing. It is sensible to launder and shrink bed ticking before making into covers if you yearn for a black-and-white striped chair cover.

Measure up your chairs carefully, armchairs vary in design and no two sides are exactly alike. In the interests of economy, measure your particular chair, finding its basic width across the back and arms, to decide the width of material you can use most economically.

To estimate the yardage, add up the lengthwise measurements, including all seam allowances,

tuck-ins. Add an extra yard for matching and placement of motifs. The total of these measurements and the width of the fabric will determine the yardage needed. Extra material is needed for gathered or pleated skirts.

Cutting out: It is easier, quicker and just as accurate to pin the material right on the chair, a section at a time.

Before cutting them to shape, check that patterns match and make sure that any design on the material is the right way up. Cut out and complete each section as you go.

Individual pieces are much easier to handle than a big slipcover bristling with pins. As each completed section is pinned to the adjacent piece the slipcover can be fitted exactly and adjusted easily.

Do all pinning and cutting on the right side of the fabric. As the two sides of an upholstered piece often differ slightly, it is necessary to pin and cut each section separately. Pin the fabric along the straight of the goods (the straight grain) and do all fitting and adjusting at this stage. Have cushions in place when pinning fabric for the placement of large motifs, so that the design can be correctly centred on different parts of the furniture.

How to measure an armchair

Measuring for yardage: Measure a sofa or upholstered chair by the method shown in the diagrams.

Step 1: On the inside back, measure from A down the inside of the sofa or chair across the seat and to the lower edge of E, add 2in for seams and allow 6in for tuck-in. For width, measure from J to N and add 2in (diag A).

Step 2: For outside back, measure from A to B, and add 2in seam for seam allowance and hem (diag B).

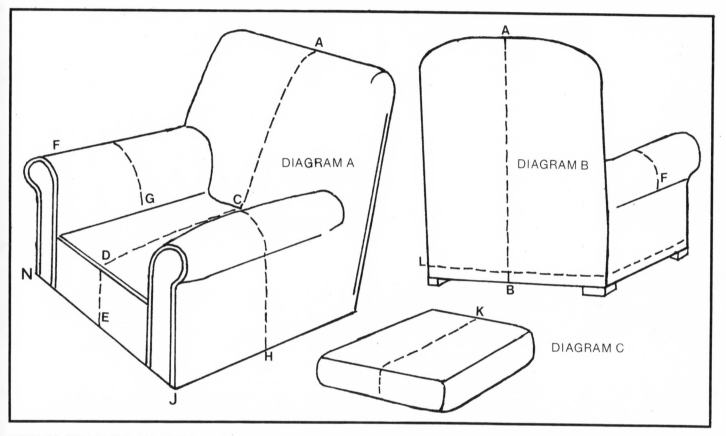

HOW TO MEASURE AN ARMCHAIR

Step 3: For outside arms, measure F, and add 2in for seam allowance and hem. Double this measurement for both arms.

Step 4: For inside arms, measure G, add 2in for seam allowance and 4in for tuck-in. Multiply by two for both arms.

Step 5: For, facing on arms, measure J, add 2in for seam allowance. Double the measurement for two arms.

Step 6: Measure width of back at base L (diag B) and width of sides outside.

Step 7: Measure sides H outside, add 2in for hem (diag A).

Step 8: Allow ½yd for flaps. These are attached to the sides, back and front of the sofa or chair to tie underneath to hide the shabby upholstery.

Step 9: Allow 1yd for piping the cover. This will give about 30yd of bias strips, ½in wide.

Step 10: Measure cushion covers and box sides allowing 1in on all seams. For back of cushion, measure top of cushion K, and double for bottom, add 1in seam allowance. Measure round the four sides for length of boxing strip. Measure depth of cushion, and allow 1in seam allowance (diag C).

Upholstery: 50" fabric, 6yds
Slip Cover: 50" fabric, 9yds
36" fabric, 12yds
Skirt: 1yd

Upholstery: 50" fabric, 8yds
Slip Cover: 50" fabric, 9½yds
36" fabric, 13yds
Skirt: 1yd

Upholstery: 50" fabric, 6yds
(Do not slip cover)

Upholstery: 50" fabric, 5yds
Slip Cover: 50" fabric, 8yds
36" fabric, 10½yds
Skirt 1½yds

Upholstery: 50" fabric, 7½yds
Slip Cover: 50" fabric, 9yds
36" fabric, 12yds
Skirt: 2yds

Upholstery: 50" fabric, 5yds
Slip Cover: 5;" fabric, 7yds
36" fabric, 9yds
Skirt: 1yd

Upholstery: 50" fabric, 5yds
Slip Cover: 50" fabric, 8yds
36" fabric, 11yds
Skirt: 1yd

Upholstery: 50" fabric, 2yds
Slip Cover: 50" fabric, 2½yds
36" fabric, 5yds

Upholstery: 50" fabric, 3yds
Slip Cover: 50" fabric, 4yds
36" fabric, 5yds
Skirt: 1½yds

Upholstery: 50" fabric, 2¼yds
Slip Cover: 50" fabric, 2½yds
36" fabric, 4½yds
Skirt: .... 1 yd

YARDAGE GUIDE FOR UPHOLSTERY AND SLIPCOVERS USING PLAIN FABRICS

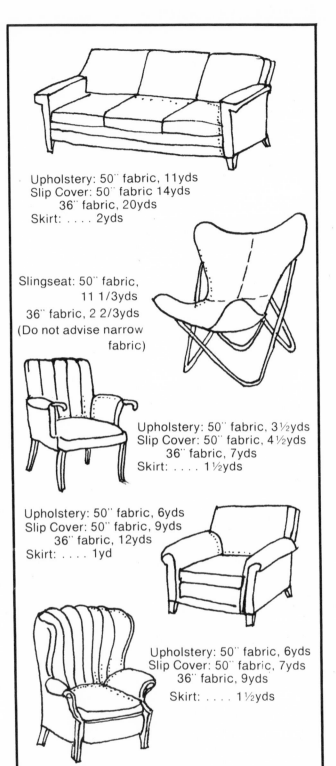

Upholstery: 50" fabric, 11yds
Slip Cover: 50" fabric 14yds
    36" fabric, 20yds
Skirt: 2yds

Slingseat: 50" fabric,
    11 1/3yds
36" fabric, 2 2/3yds
(Do not advise narrow
    fabric)

Upholstery: 50" fabric, 3½yds
Slip Cover: 50" fabric, 4½yds
    36" fabric, 7yds
Skirt: 1½yds

Upholstery: 50" fabric, 6yds
Slip Cover: 50" fabric, 9yds
    36" fabric, 12yds
Skirt: 1yd

Upholstery: 50" fabric, 6yds
Slip Cover: 50" fabric, 7yds
    36" fabric, 9yds
Skirt: 1½yds

YARDAGE CHART FOR SLIPCOVERS

Type	Cushions	48in Wide		36in Wide		Piping or Trimming
		Plain	Figured or Striped	Plain	Figured or Striped	
Sofa	2-3	14	15½	21	23	36
6-7ft	1 Lge	13½	15	20½	22½	33
	0	10	11	15	17	21
3ft sectional						
1 arm	1	6½	7½	12	12½	25
no arm	1	5	6	11	11½	20
Sofa bed	2	14½	16	20	21	40
Love seat	2	10½	12½	15	16½	24
	1	10½	11	15	16½	23
	0	8½	9½	13	14½	14
Arm chair	1	7½	8¼	11¼	12¼	18
Club chair	0	6½	7	8½	9½	13
Wing chair	1	8	9	12	13½	18
	0	6½	7¼	9¾	10¾	13
Boudoir	1	5	6½	8	9	15
chair	0	4½	5½	6½	7½	12
Dining room chair	0	1½	1¾	1⅚	2⅙	5½
Daybed and	3	14½	16	21¾	23¾	42
mattress	0	11	12	17½	19½	27
Daybed	3	11	12	16½	18	29
	0	7½	8¼	11	12¼	14
Extra cushion	1	1¼	1¾	2	2¼	5

Note: Always check with sales assistant if pattern is large.

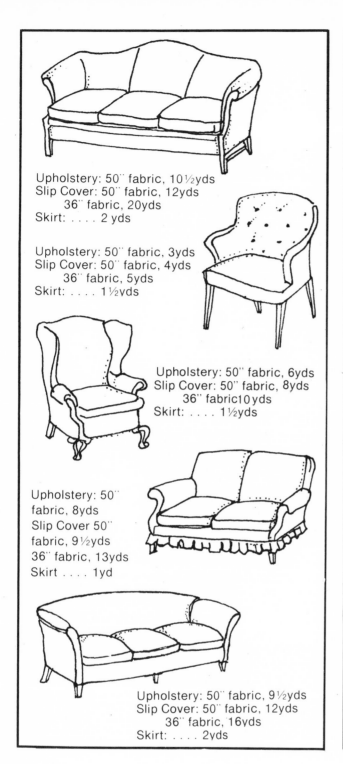

Upholstery: 50" fabric, 10½yds
Slip Cover: 50" fabric, 12yds
  36" fabric, 20yds
Skirt: . . . . 2 yds

Upholstery: 50" fabric, 3yds
Slip Cover: 50" fabric, 4yds
  36" fabric, 5yds
Skirt: 1½yds

Upholstery: 50" fabric, 6yds
Slip Cover: 50" fabric, 8yds
  36" fabric10yds
Skirt: 1½yds

Upholstery: 50"
fabric, 8yds
Slip Cover 50"
fabric, 9½yds
36" fabric, 13yds
Skirt 1yd

Upholstery: 50" fabric, 9½yds
Slip Cover: 50" fabric, 12yds
  36" fabric, 16yds
Skirt: 2yds

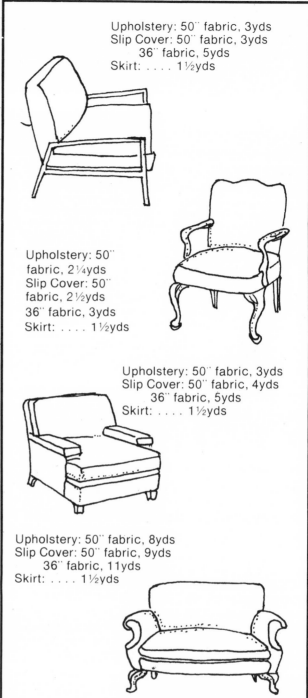

Upholstery: 50" fabric, 3yds
Slip Cover: 50" fabric, 3yds
  36" fabric, 5yds
Skirt: 1½yds

Upholstery: 50"
fabric, 2¼yds
Slip Cover: 50"
fabric, 2½yds
36" fabric, 3yds
Skirt: 1½yds

Upholstery: 50" fabric, 3yds
Slip Cover: 50" fabric, 4yds
  36" fabric, 5yds
Skirt: 1½yds

Upholstery: 50" fabric, 8yds
Slip Cover: 50" fabric, 9yds
  36" fabric, 11yds
Skirt: 1½yds

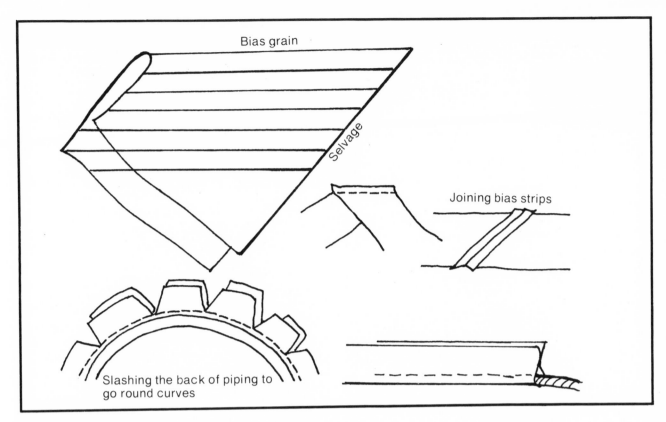

Bias grain

Selvage

Joining bias strips

Slashing the back of piping to
go round curves

HOW TO MAKE PIPING

How to make piping

Piping is used for decorative purposes on bedspreads and cushions, but on loose covers it serves
two purposes: one is decorative, the other is to
strengthen the seams of the cover at the weakest
points.

Material for piping is cut on the cross. Piping
cord available from haberdashery counters and
curtain departments of stores should be boiled and
pre-shrunk before covering it with the material.

For an average size easy chair with loose
cushions, 12-14yds of piping may be needed and a
sofa with three cushions could take 25yds.

Cut a yard of 36in material, on the bias, into
1½in wide strips; if using a heavier cord, the
strips will need to be made wider. Join the strips
together with stitching on the lengthwise grain
and press the seams open. Join together to make
one long strip, this is easier to work with and you
can cut off the lengths as required.

Fold material down the centre, lay the cord in the
fold and stitch close to the cord using the piping
foot on your machine. Stretch the bias material
slightly as you work. Roll the completed cord round
a piece of cardboard for easy handling. When
sewing piping to curved shapes, slash the back
of the piping to go round the curves (see diagrams).

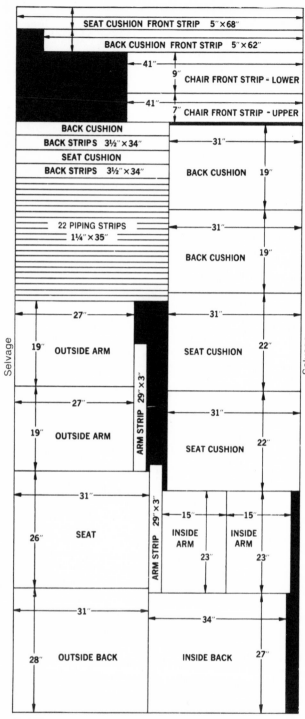

**FABRIC LAYOUT—ADJUST MEASUREMENTS
FOR YOUR CHAIR**

The following labels appear within the fabric layout diagram:

- SEAT CUSHION FRONT STRIP 5" × 68"
- BACK CUSHION FRONT STRIP 5" × 62"
- 41"
- 9" CHAIR FRONT STRIP - LOWER
- 41"
- 7" CHAIR FRONT STRIP - UPPER
- BACK CUSHION
- BACK STRIPS 3½" × 34"
- SEAT CUSHION
- BACK STRIPS 3½" × 34"
- 22 PIPING STRIPS 1¼" × 35"
- 31"
- BACK CUSHION 19"
- 31"
- BACK CUSHION 19"
- Selvage
- 27"
- 19" OUTSIDE ARM
- ARM STRIP 29" × 3"
- 31"
- SEAT CUSHION 22"
- 27"
- 19" OUTSIDE ARM
- 31"
- SEAT CUSHION 22"
- Selvage
- 31"
- 26" SEAT
- ARM STRIP 29" × 3"
- 15"
- INSIDE ARM 23"
- 15"
- INSIDE ARM 23"
- 31"
- 28" OUTSIDE BACK
- 34"
- INSIDE BACK 27"

To Slipcover a Large Club Chair

The simplest way to give new life to a large arm chair is to fit a new slipcover in one of the attractive designs now available in furnishing fabrics. Period designs are suitable and popular.

Materials: Brown paper or large sheets of news-paper for patterns; transparent adhesive tape to join pattern pieces together where necessary; length of tape to go round base of chair; press studs or slide fasteners.

To measure the exact amount of fabric required for chair: First make the pattern pieces using diagrams 1 and 2 as your guide. The pieces shown in diagram 1 are: A, inside back (allow 6in to tuck down into back of seat); B, chair seat (allow 6in at the back and on either side to tuck away); C, front of seat; D, arm roll (this piece goes right over the arm, starting just below the seat level inside, and ending on the outside at the point shown in diagram 2); E, scroll.

Pattern pieces for the back of the chair (diag 2) are: F, outside arm; G, outside back; H, border strip. If there is a loose seat cushion, make two patterns, one for the top and one for the bottom of the cover and another pattern for the inset or boxing strip (the long strip round the sides connecting the top to the bottom cover).

For the skirt measure round the chair allowing an extra 16in for inverted pleats. Depth will be from bottom of chair to floor.

When you have cut all the pattern pieces, measure and mark the space on the floor 48in wide and 3yd long. Pretend this is a piece of fabric and on it place the pieces. Allow double the area for each piece, as they will either be cut twice or placed on the fold. Allow 1in round the outside of each piece for seams and 1½in for lower hems on pieces C, F, and G. Each time you fill the 48in by 3yd space you will need 3yd of fabric; add an extra yard of fabric for the facings.

Cushion covers: Allow 1in seam allowance. Cut out cushion cover pieces and sew one long edge of inset to the top of cushion cover, the right sides facing and the raw edges level. Where they meet join narrow edges of inset and trim off surplus fabric.

Sew the other long edge of inset round the bottom of the cover, starting on one side 2in from the end and finishing on the opposite side in the same position. This leaves an opening through which to insert the cushion.

Cut a piece of fabric for the facing (this is the flap attached to one edge of the cushion cover opening and it tucks between the cushion and the cover avoiding the need for a slide fastener). This facing will be the same width as the boxing strip and the length of the opening, plus 3in at either end.

Sew one long edge of the facing to the free edge of the bottom cover, right sides together and raw edges level, and leave the 3in overlap free on either side. Sew the lower edges of the 3in overlaps along the seam lines of bottom cover and inset. Neatly hemstitch raw edges of inset and facing.

Chair cover: Cut out the pieces for the chair cover as follows: from single fabric, cut two pieces each for D, E, and F; cut remaining pieces A, B, C, G, H from double fabric, placing the straight edge of each piece (the centre line of the chair) on the fold.

All shaping is done directly on the chair, by pinning each piece of cover on the appropriate part of the chair, right side of fabric outside.

Fit inside back (A) snugly at each top corner of chair by pinning darts. (Make a dart by pinching fabric to fit, then pin the fold into dart shape. Each dart will be about ¾in to 1in wide and only a few inches long.)

Shape outside back (G) to outline of chair, leave 1in all round edge for turnings and trim off surplus fabric.

Where outside back curves over the back of the arm roll, carefully slash the fabric so it fits into the shallow hollow between back and arm, but leave about ½in seam allowance unslashed.

Pin on seat piece (B) pushing the three tuckaway sides well down into the crevices of the chair, and shaping the piece to fit the chair seat. Pin on the rest of the pieces, shaping them to fit, and pin hem along lower edges of pieces C, F, and G. Mark seamlines with pins or tailor's chalk—arm roll (D), inside back (A) and seat piece (B) will be joined along their tuckaway edges. Remove cover pieces from the chair and stitch the darts.

Stitch all the seams (right sides facing, raw edges level) except side seams which join the outside back to outside arm, arm roll and part of border strip. Seam the tuckaway edges of arm roll, inside back and seat pieces with a double row of stitching, leaving ¼in between each row—this strengthens the seams.

Stitch hems on pieces C, F, and G and through this continuous hem run a tape. When cover is placed on chair, the tape is drawn up and tied out of sight round one back leg.

To make plackets to fasten the cover, trim the seam allowance down each side opening to ½in, clipping in towards the stitching where the opening meets the top seam—this gives a smooth, non-wrinkle finish.

Cut four strips of fabric, two of them 4½in wide, the others 3in wide, each as long as the opening, plus 1in. Stitch narrow strips to the open edges of the outside back, wider strips to the other sides of the openings. In each case keep right sides of fabric facing and raw edges level and leave ½in overlap at each narrow end of the strips. Turn each overlap to the wrong side and tack. Turn under ½in raw edges of strips and tack. Cut the skirt to fit across the back, the other piece goes round three sides. Hem the skirt.

Attach back skirt separately to back piece, hem sides.

Slipstitch folded edges of strips to wrong side of cover along the seam lines. On the outside back, turn in plackets; slipstitch to wrong side; sew press studs on all plackets at 4in intervals—the narrow plackets tuck round the back of the chair under plackets on outside back.

Sew the rest of the skirt piece to the chair cover.

Fit cover on chair. Push the tuckaway seams into the side and back crevices. To hold these in place push a roll of newspaper tightly into each crevice or use cardboard cylinders, such as used for calendars and pictures, deep into the crevices to hold the covers in place.

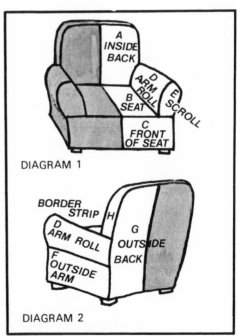

DIAGRAM 1

DIAGRAM 2

HOW TO MEASURE FOR A CLUB CHAIR

If you are using a patterned fabric when slip covering a large club chair make sure you place the design so it blends to best advantage with the pattern on surrounding pieces.

To Make a Slipcover From Stretch Fabric

Now that the new stretch fabrics are available, making slipcovers is much easier than it used to be. The stretch in the fabric allows you to fit the cover more snugly over curves and retains shape so well that you can give your sewing a professional looking finish.

Stretch fabrics are readily available and most are 60in wide so they cut economically. Another advantage is that there is no need to cut fabric on the bias for piping.

When working out yardage, remember the loops of the knit should all run in the same direction. Find the end that does not ravel and use that for the bottom of the slipcover pieces.

With a tape measure level with the bottom of the chair at the back, bring tape up over back, down to the seat, across the seat down to the bottom of the front of the chair. This total measurement will give the length of fabric required.

To cut stretch fabric use long, even strokes and sharp, firm scissors.

Prevent ravelling of the cut pieces by stay-stitching each piece with a straight machine stitch ¼in from cut edges. Use a polyester or nylon thread and a size 14 needle for the machine sewing. Stitch length should be 12 stitches per inch on straight seams, and 15 stitches per inch on curves. If your machine has it, use the stretch stitch.

Piping can be the same fabric or a contrast stretch fabric, but make sure that it has the same wearing and laundering properties as the slipcover.

To cut out:
Inside back (piece 1, diag 1 and 2): Remove back cushion if any. Lay fabric right side up on the chair back. Pin the fabric to the chair and make a chalk mark along the seam line on the top edge of the chair. Allow ½in seam allowance beyond this line

and cut out the shape. The seams where the inside back of the slipcover joins the inside wing pieces require fabric allowance for tucking in to ensure a smooth fit.

To do this, taper the cut from the ½in seam allow-

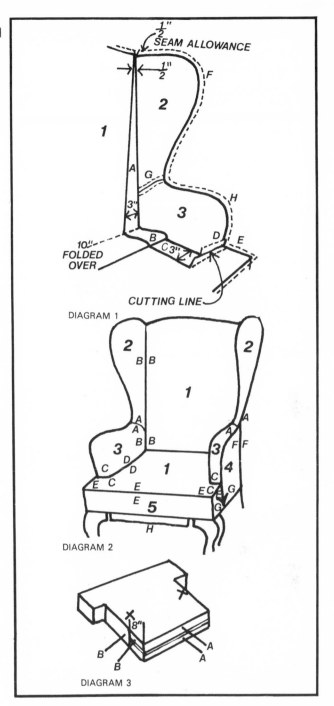

DIAGRAM 1

DIAGRAM 2

DIAGRAM 3

TO MAKE A SLIPCOVER FROM STRETCH FABRIC

ance at the top edge to 3in, tuck in allowance where the back and the seat meet (A—diag 1). Fold over 10in of fabric to be used for tucking between chair back and seat (B—diag 1). Carry the fabric across the seat, allowing 3in between chair arms and the sides of the seat (C—diag 1).

To prevent fabric moving, pin firmly to chair seat. Where the arm front meets the chair seat, discontinue the tuck-in allowance and cut fabric straight with ½in seam allowance beyond the seam line that joins the seat cover to the arm fronts (D—diag 1). Allow ½in for seams and cut fabric along the outside edges of the seat, side and front (E—diag 1).

Inside wing (piece 2, diag 1 and 2): With right side of fabric facing, pin to top inside wing surface. Mark with chalk along seam edge on outside curve of wing (F—diag 1) and seam line where wing and arm pieces join (G—diag 1). Allow ½in seam allowance beyond the seam line where wing joins back, with same tapering tuck-in allowances as used on the back pieces.

Inside arm (piece 3, diag 1 and 2): Pin on fabric and mark with chalk along the seam line for joining the wing and arm piece (G—diag 1) and along outside edge of the arm (H—diag 1). Allow ½in seam allowances and cut fabric. With chalk, mark seam joining seat to front edge of arm (D—diag 1). Allow ½in seam allowance and cut. Continue the cutting line for 3in to provide same tuck-in allowance as that on chair seat piece. Cut back edge of arm piece to correspond with tuck-in allowance on side seam of back piece.

Outside wings and arm (piece 4, diag 2): Pin fabric to the chair. Make a chalk mark along the seam line where outside back and sides join. Allow ½in seam allowance beyond the chalk marked line down to where the arms join the chair. At this point increase the seam allowance to 1in to take the slide fastener inserted for closing. You need an opening on at least one side of the slipcover to slip on and off easily.

Mark with chalk the seam line that will join the outside piece (4—diag 2) to the inside wing and arm piece (2, 3—diag 2). Allow ½in seam allowance and cut fabric. Continue cutting line straight down from front edge of chair arm to bottom of chair to make the chair seat (G—diag 2). Cut fabric ½in below bottom edge of chair.

Front edge piece (piece 5, diag 2): Pin fabric to front surface of chair and around the sides (G—diag 2). Mark fabric at seam G line, and at top and bottom edge of chair front and sides. Allow ½in seam allowance on all marked lines then cut fabric.

Outside back:
Pin fabric to the chair back. With chalk, mark along seam line where outside back and sides join, cut fabric allowing ½in seam allowance. Mark the inside seams with chalk then cut, allowing ½in seam allowance. Allow ½in fabric below bottom edge of chair and cut.

To make up:
Join the inside wing piece (2) and inside arm piece (3) together at seam A (diag 2). Next join this piece (2, 3) to inside back piece (1), starting at the top and working down to where the seat joins the sides and back.

Reverse the work and sew seam C (diag 2) joining the arm front to the seat. Continue sewing these pieces together (seam D) until it meets seam B. Ease in any excess tuck-in allowance fullness where all the pieces join. Trim if necessary to make a smoother, neater seam. Sew in the slide fastener.

On pattern piece 4, stitch one side of the slide fastener tape to the 1in allowance. Make sure fastener is positioned close enough to what would have been the seam line so that when it is closed the side and back pieces will fit snugly together as if they had been sewn.

Stitch piping made from 1in wide fabric cut on the cross to side seam allowances of outside back pieces. Join the piped outside back piece to outside side pieces (4) starting at the top and continuing until you reach the slide fastener stitched into the side piece.

Fit the back and side pieces on the chair again and pin the other side of the slide fastener in position so that the two pieces line up for a good, smooth fit. Join front piece (5) to edges of seat (seam E). Pipe this seam as you sew.

Pin piping to the piece that will cover the chair back and sides.

After piping is sewn, pin this piece to the assembled front pieces and sew together. Ease fullness round curves of wings and arm edges. The piped seam continues down outside front arm edge (seam G) to bottom of chair.

Finish bottom edge with piping on all sides. On each of the four sides sew a 1½in strip of fabric to bottom edge of slipcover between the chair legs (H) and sew strings to the centre of each piece. These tie under the chair seat and hold the cover in position.

To finish the bottom of the chair, cut a frill the depth from front of chair to floor and three times the distance round the chair. Hem bottom and gather to chair cover in knife pleats or gathers as desired.

Sew in position and cover join with piping.

Lightly press wrong side of slipcover with steam iron, then press right side. The setting on the iron should be the temperature of the fibre having the lowest heat tolerance if the fabric is a blend of more than one fibre.

Covering a T-cushion
The T-shaped cushion is the one usually used on wing chairs.

Bedspreads are fun to make. This throw-over bedspread can be varied from its basic style with trimming.

Take a cushion from the chair and lay the fabric on the cushion. Mark around the edges with chalk to get your shape. Make ½in seam allowance. Cut one piece for the top, the other for the bottom. For width of boxing strip (the piece of fabric that goes around the cushion), measure the cushion from top to bottom and allow 1in extra.

The cushion cover is closed with a slide fastener to make it easy to take the cushion in and out for laundering or dry cleaning. For this section of the boxing strip, measure the width of the cushion across the back and add 17in. Cut two strips this length in the width you decided for the boxing strip.

Measure 8in from the back corner along one side (X—diag 3) around the front of the cushion to a point X, 8in from the opposite back corner on the other side. Add 1in to this figure for seam allowances then cut a strip of fabric this length in the width of the boxing strip.

Fold the two back boxing strips in half, lengthwise. Place the folded edges together and tack the slide fastener in position (A—diag 3). Next sew in the slide fastener, then stitch this back strip to the front strip using the ½in seam allowance (B—diag 3).

Sew piping to the top and bottom edges of this boxing strip. Then sew the top and bottom cushion pieces to the boxing strip with ½in seams, with right sides facing. Open slide fastener and turn cushion to right side.

Sewing hints when using stretch material
Polyester double knit can be stitched on either a straight-stitch or a zigzag-stitch machine. It requires a looser tension than you generally use and, possibly, less pressure on the presser foot to ensure a smooth, unpuckered seam.

If top layer ripples, pressure is too heavy and must be loosened. If fabric does not feed properly, pressure may be too light; tighten pressure regulator.

If seam is puckered, tension is too tight; loosen top tension and bobbin screw.

If stitch is not balanced, loosen tension on the side where the stitching is tighter.

If you have made an adjustment, cut off test-seam; repeat tests and adjustments until seam is satisfactory.

Slipcover for a Bedroom Chair

Slipcover for a bedroom chair
A bright slipcover, made from luxurious silk or similar, can give a shabby bedroom chair a new lease of life.

The slipcover is made in two pieces:
(1) Make a pattern of the seat and back in calico or old sheeting for easy handling.

(2) Take the measurement for the chair skirt and double it for the desired fullness. Add extra for hems and turnings.

Estimate the amount of fabric needed for seat and back, and add ⅓yd extra for cutting bias strips for covering piping cord.

You will also need piping cord, a long slide fastener for the back opening, taped snap fasteners for the back of the skirt, a roll of ¾in wide white tape, a large hook and eye.

To make:
Step 1: Using calico pattern, cut out seat shape. Place on the seat right side out and pin fit.

Step 2: Trim the corners, leaving ample allowance for seams.

Step 3: Stitch the two front corners only (diag A)

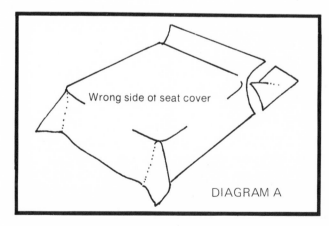

Wrong side of seat cover

DIAGRAM A

and leave the back ones unstitched. Make two separate pieces and join to the unstitched back corners (diag B) to make the skirt into one complete unit.

Step 4: Sew covered piping to the lower edges of the

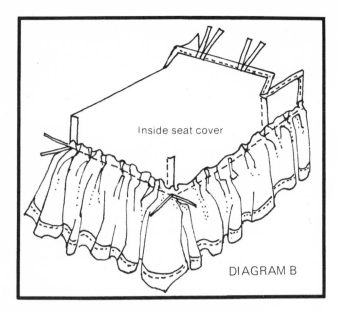

Inside seat cover

DIAGRAM B

For the final finish

At right are some decorative ideas for trimming slipcover skirts to give an additional professional finish.

Recovering Dining Chairs

Give a new lease of life to jaded dining chairs. Cover the seats with vinyl and add a matching backrest.

Measure chair seat and width and depth of back rest. This will give you the amount of fabric needed for one chair. Multiply by the number of chairs you plan to cover to get total yardage. Allow 1in for turnings.

Turn chair upside-down and make sure that any springs and broken webbing are repaired before starting to cover the seat. Cut a paper pattern of the chair seat and fit it to the chair before cutting fabric. Cut out fabric, allowing 1in turnings.

Place on chair and, starting at the front, tack cover under chair with upholstery nails. Pull fabric tight and tack the back section under chair with nails. Next tack one side in the same way under the chair and then the other side, pulling the fabric taut, so that it lies smoothly over the chair seat.

To finish seat, fringe lengths of vinyl and tack to the front and sides of seat with upholstery nails. Choose nails with heads to match vinyl or heads with a metal finish for contrast.

For chair back, cut fabric to fit snugly across back. Tack top to rail then down the sides, making sure that it is taut. Trim with fringe across the bottom.

Upholstery braid may be used instead of fringe. Use fabric glue to attach braid.

See illustration page 130.

seat shape. Pin skirt to seat, gathering or box pleating as desired so that it fits neatly. Stitch skirt in position, level the hem, sew on tapes, neaten edges.

Step 5: Using calico pattern, cut seat back. Pin fit with fabric right side out. Take a long dart in the back to allow for slide fastener. Mark seam lines, slip the cover off.

Step 6: Slash dart on the chair back. Insert slide fastener upside down, using the cording foot. Stitch the two back pieces together.

Step 7: Turn cover to right side, fit over chair back. Sew tapes, fasteners, hook and eye (diag C).

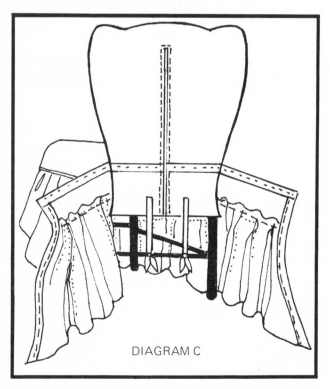

DIAGRAM C

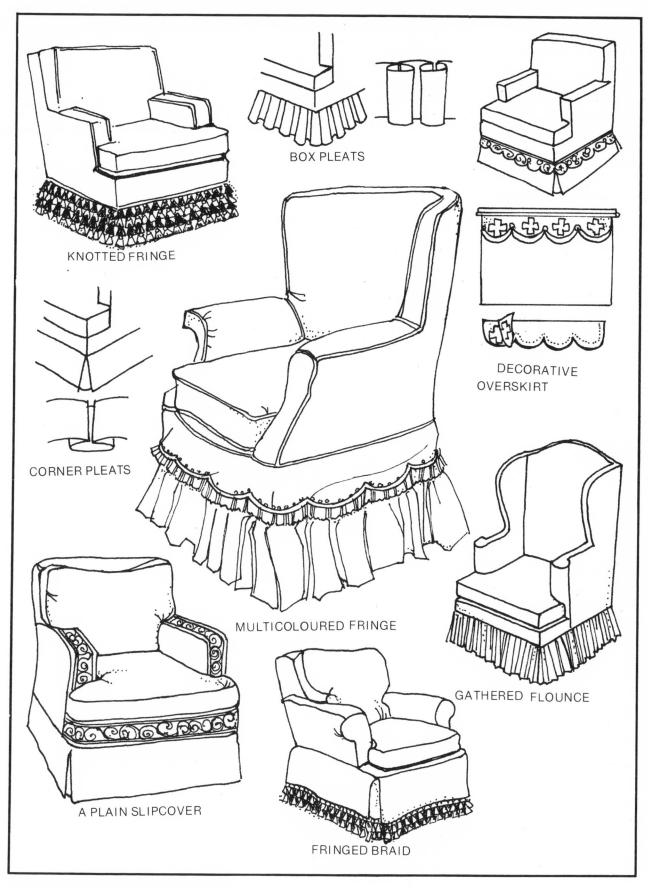

BOX PLEATS

KNOTTED FRINGE

DECORATIVE
OVERSKIRT

CORNER PLEATS

MULTICOLOURED FRINGE

GATHERED FLOUNCE

A PLAIN SLIPCOVER

FRINGED BRAID

SLIP COVER FOR THE FINAL FINISH

Vinyl fabrics

The look of beautifully tanned leathers has been faked so well today that only an expert tanner can tell the difference. Vinyl fabrics are very popular for upholstery and furniture coverings, so if you plan to use vinyl fabrics here is an illustrated guide for the yardage needed for different types of chair shapes. Yardages are based on 54in wide vinyls.

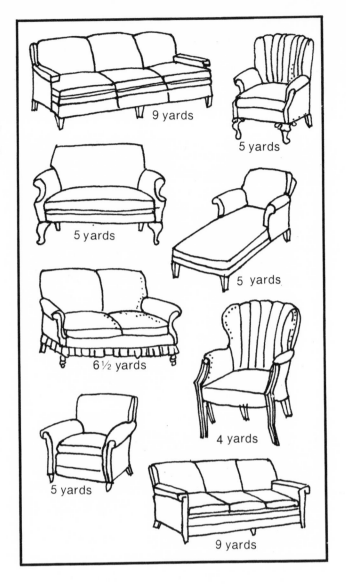

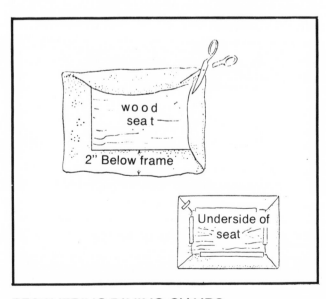

RECOVERING DINING CHAIRS

9 yards

2 ¾ yards

4 yards

1 yard

5 yards

5 yards

4 yards

2 yards

4 yards

9 yards

2 ¾ yards

9 yards

5 yards

5 yards

8 yards

4 yards

YARDAGE CHART FOR VINYL FABRICS

How to Make Box Cushion Covers

Loose cushions are widely used on modern furniture, so it is helpful to know an easy method for making box cushion covers and the economical way to lay out fabric.

Measure your cushions, and adapt the directions given.

To make: The covers for a set of four box cushions, each 3in deep and 18in square, will need 2¾yd of 48in strong furnishing fabric.

Step 1: Use the fabric layout shown and cut your fabric according to this diagram. There is ½in allowance for turnings throughout.

Step 2: To form the box sides of the cushion covers, take two strips of fabric, each 37in by 4in wide. Make two seams by stitching the shorter edges together (allow ½in turnings). Press seams open.

Step 3: With the right side of the fabric outside, measure 1in from a seam and make a 16in cut lengthways, and then tack and stitch the slide fastener in place.

Step 4: Allowing ½in turnings, tack the front and back of the cushion to the side panel, making sure that the two seams on the panel are placed at the corners for neatness. Stitch, then press open the seams. Turn the covers and insert the foam cushion.

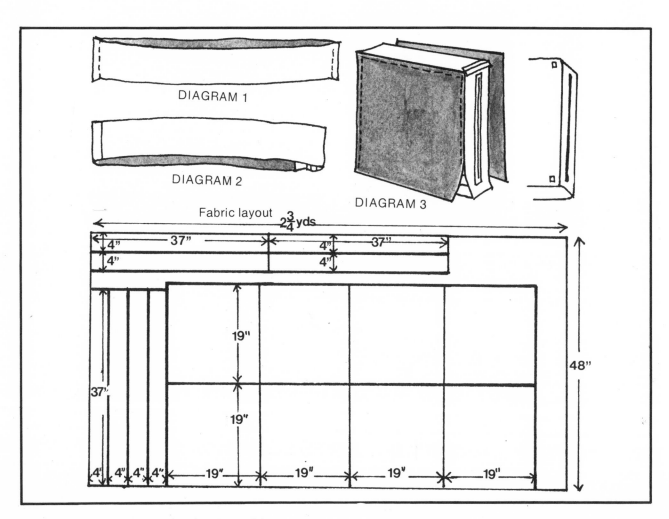

DIAGRAM 1

DIAGRAM 2

DIAGRAM 3

Fabric layout 2¾yds

4" 37" 4" 37"

4" 4"

19"

19"

37"

48"

4" 4" 4" 4" 19" 19" 19" 19"

HOW TO MAKE BOX CUSHION COVERS

A boxed cushion can add colour and comfort to many types of chairs.

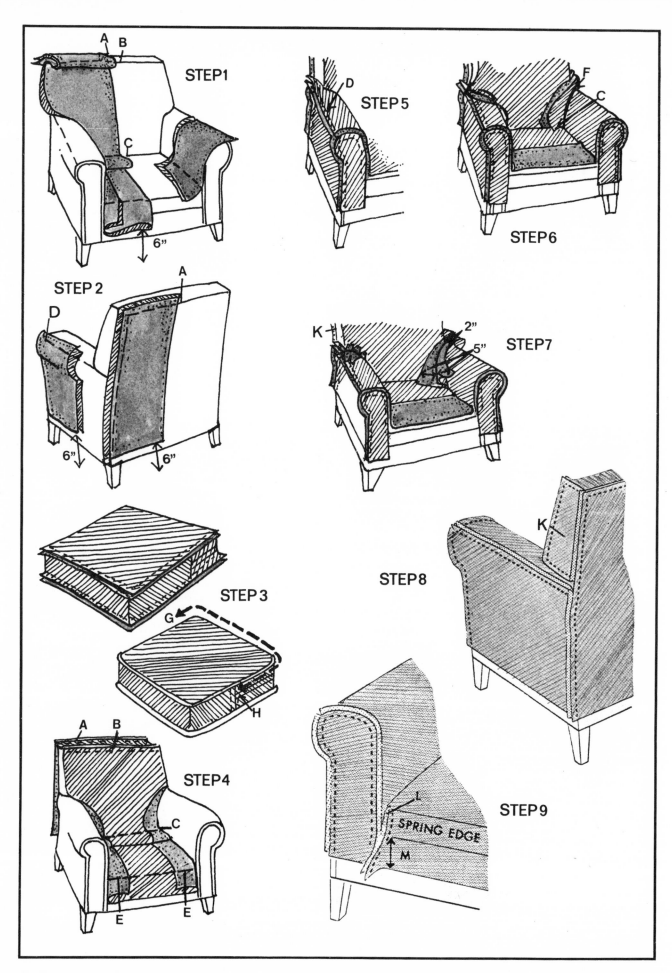

STEP 1

A B

C

6"

STEP 2

A

D

6" 6"

STEP 3

G

H

STEP 4

A B

C

E E

STEP 5

D

STEP 6

F

C

STEP 7

K 2"

5"

STEP 8

K

STEP 9

L

SPRING EDGE

M

SLIPCOVER A CHAIR

Slipcover a Chair With Plain Fabric (Another Method)

When using plain fabric or all over print pin the fabric on the chair a section at a time.

1. **Inside back:** Fold fabric in half lengthwise starting 2in below the back of the chair (A), bring fabric forward across the top to (B). Fold in 2in for a piping seam then continue down the back of the chair to inside seat (C). Fold in 10in to allow for a 5in tuck-in at the back of the seat. Continue across the seat and down to 6in above the floor, cut straight across the fabric. (Diag step 1)

Inside arms: Fold fabric in half lengthwise starting 2in beyond where the chair arm starts to turn down, smooth fabric over arm and down to the seat (C) and allow 5in tuck-in. Cut straight across fabric. Repeat for the other arm.

2. **Outside back:** Fold fabric in half lengthwise and starting at (A) which is 2in above top back of chair continue down the back of the chair to 6in from the floor. Cut straight across the fabric. The skirt is cut out later. (Diag step 2)

Outside arms: Fold fabric in half lengthwise and starting 2in above (D), where the arm starts to turn down, smooth the fabric and hold it close under the curve of the arm and against the side of the chair until it is 6in from the floor. Cut straight across the fabric. Repeat for the other arm. Front and side panels are cut later when you start pinning the pieces together.

3. **Cushion:** If your chair has a loose cushion remove from the chair and lay it on top of your folded fabric. Draw round the cushion shape with a piece of chalk allowing 1in seam all round. Cut out. Cushion may be slightly uneven so measure the boxing strip (cushion band) at widest and narrowest points. Get an average width for the band by dividing this total in half. Allow 2in for seams. Cut one band of correct width from G to H around the front and add 4in for finishing the ends. Cut two more bands the same width and length to go around the cushion back to take the slide fastener.

3A. **To make up the cushion:** Fold two bands in half lengthwise and pin each along the fold.

Sew one band to the cushion top at G and around the back to H with the folded edge down. Stitch the other band to the bottom of the cushion in the same position with the folded edge upwards. Sew slide fastener between the folded edges from G to H. (If the cushion is T-shape extend the back bands for the fastener to the beginning of T on one side to allow easy insertion of the cushion.) Turn under the ends of the front band for 1in and attach to the top and bottom of the cushion front from G to H. Overlap the ends for a smooth finish. (Diag step 3)

4. **To make the cover:** Place inside back fabric on chair. Pin a 1in seam at B for the piping then cut through this fold of fabric. Pin the front back and outside back together at (A). Fold a 5in tuck-in at (C). Smooth the fabric over the chair seat and down the front. Fold back the excess fabric (E) and allowing 5in for inside arm tuck-ins, cut to back of chair. (If chair has a T-shaped front, do not cut the front piece but only the fabric inside arm. The extra will go around the T to meet the panel or outside arm.) (Diag step 4)

5. **The arms:** Be sure that the outside arm piece is smoothed close under the curve of the arm. Pin to the chair under the curve at front and back to hold firm. Pin outside and inside arm pieces together. Begin at front where the arm begins to slope down D and continue in straight line along the arm to back of chair. Pin outside arm and back together. With fabric on straight grain of goods, pin in position then cut the front panel. Repeat for the other side. (Diag step 5)

6. Smooth the inside arm into the crease where arm meets back. Chalk fabric along crease from C where the back, arm and the seat meet to point F where arm and back meet. Cut away excess fabric beginning 2in on the far side of F and taper down to 5in from chalk mark at C. Repeat on the other side. Smooth the inside back into crease and follow the instructions just given for the two sides. Be sure to cut on the near side of the chalk mark. (Diag step 6)

7. Stand facing the chair with scissors pointed toward the back of the chair. Clip the fabric about four times 2in apart with alternate left and right slants until it lies smoothly around the curve where back and arm join. Be very careful not to clip too close to the seam. Three or four clips should be ample. Repeat for the other inside back and both arm pieces. (Diag step 7)

8. Carry the remaining piece of the inside arm back and pin to outside back. Pin the inside arm and inside back together from C to F as in Step 6. This forms the tuck-in that goes into the

chair crease. Repeat on the other side. With fabric on the straight of grain, cut, fit and pin the side panels K. Pin the bottom edge of panel to inside arm piece. (Diag step 8)

9. If the chair has a sprung edge that bounces up and down at the front edge of the chair avoid any pull on the arm fabric by first pushing the seat tuck-in down between the spring edge and the arm. Mitre the corner with a dart (L) and cut away the excess fabric. Push the inside arm tuck-in down between the spring edge and the arm and pin to front arm panel. Pin front of chair and arm panel together from the bottom of spring edge to bottom of fabric M. (Diag step 9)

A pretty bedroom chair covered in brocade.

A beautifully patterned slipcover gives an elegant touch to this chair.

Bedspreads and other Bedroom Accessories

Graceful bedroom furniture can be had quite inexpensively by providing frilled draperies on a dressing table or re-covering a bedroom stool in a brightly coloured fabric. Decorative headboards can add a distinctive note to a plain bedhead.

Bedspreads are fun to make. You must start by following some basic rules but then you can let your imagination run riot. We have included directions for basic types of spreads here but you can add endless variations to produce exciting and unusual effects.

Bedspreads

Important measurements: Begin by taking measurements when the bed is made up with blankets and sheets in place, since these will increase the size of the bed. Measure top length, top width, side overhang, foot overhang, head overhang, depth of top mattress, top of box spring to floor and 'returns' at head overhang. Armed with these measurements it will be possible for you to make any type of spread.

'Return at head overhang' refers to beds with headboards. It is an extension of the side treatment at the head end, and rounds the corners to run 6 to 10in in along the headboard, holding the side overhang in place. If a bed does not have headboards, but the head end is against the wall, the return is also used.

To the measurements add ½in for each seam allowance and 2in for hems. If the pillow is to be covered by the spread add 30in to the top length measurement to allow for pillow covering and tuck-in. When planning your yardage requirements, always place the full width of the fabric down

the centre of the bed. Then any necessary piecing can be done on either side.

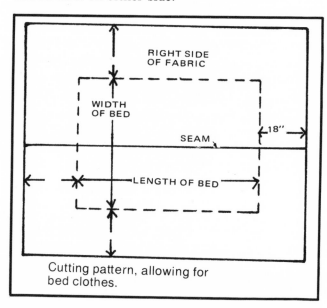

Cutting pattern, allowing for bed clothes.

MEASUREMENTS FOR A BEDSPREAD

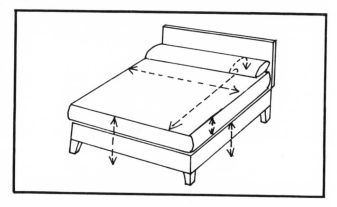

A Throwover Bedspread

The throwover bedspread is the simplest and easiest of all to make. Choose your favourite plain colour that will tone with the rest of the room or choose a patterned fabric to match a set of curtains.

For a single bed use 36in fabric, for a double bed 48in or 54in fabric. If you use the wider fabric no seam down the centre will be needed. You will need 6yd of either width. Cut your fabric into two lengths of 3yd each. If using plain fabric avoid a seam down the centre. Lay one piece down the centre of the bed. Cut the remaining piece in two lengthwise and join a length to each

side of the centre strip. Round off the corners and hem or trim with fringe or braid.

If using a floral or printed fabric a centre seam will be better since you can cut the fabric design to match when seamed together down the centre.

Measure the bed with the bedding in place. If using a sheer fabric be sure to line the spread so that the blanket will not show through.

A Tailored Bedspread

The bedspread is the dominant decorating theme in the bedroom so it will provide the focal point in your colour scheme. You can make it frilly and feminine or trim and tailored. Choose a fabric that will not wrinkle readily.

To work out the amount of material needed for the spread, make up the bed first. Measure the bed from head to foot and continue to the point where you plan to end the spread, then add a little extra for finishing the edges. This gives you the figure for one length.

For width, measure the bed across the top. Then measure from edge of the bed to the point where you plan to end the spread; double this figure and add it to the one you got across the top of the bed. This gives the width needed. Add all measurements together for yardage.

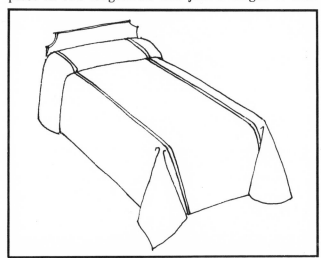

THROWOVER BEDSPREAD

Allow half inch for seams on centre and side panels and 2½in for bottom hem. For braid yardage measure round top of bed and along side panels where you plan to trim the bedspread. Add all measurements together for yardage.

Cut two pieces of fabric the length and width of the bed (54in fabric will not need joining). Place one length as a panel directly down the centre of the bed. Split the other strip lengthwise for the two side panels. Cut another strip for foot of the bed, same depth as side panels and 16in wider than bed for box pleat allowance.

Stitch side panels to each end of bottom panel, forming inverted box pleats at corners, using 8in of bottom panel for each pleat. Attach side and bottom panels to centre top panel. If using piping, insert between side and top panels as you sew. Turn up hem all around.

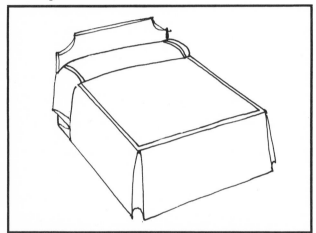

TAILORED BEDSPREAD WITH BOX-PLEATED CORNERS

Shortie Bedcover with Permanent Valance

A very pretty cover and easier to make than it looks. The valance may be gathered or box pleated and is permanently fixed to the bed; the little cover is simply thrown over it.

Valance: This can be made from any type of material. Be generous with fullness, especially with sheers. Allow twice the measurement, or even more, around three sides of the bed to make the fullness attractive. Linens, heavy cottons and chintzes may be box-pleated.

Sew the ruffle to an old sheet or a piece of strong calico the size of the mattress top. If pleating, try to arrange the pleats to fall in the same position at each corner. If gathering sheers, equalize the gathers to make an attractive flounce.

The ruffle, valance or skirt, as it is sometimes called, is fitted to the bed permanently over the springs. All you need to cover the bed is a shortie bedcover that will reach to the top of the ruffles or pleats. This can be made as a simple throwover, with either a plain or scalloped hem or a contrast border. Make a paper pattern for the scallops before cutting the material. If fabric is sheer or fairly thin, such as chintz, it is best to line the cover for a richer appearance.

If cover is to be interlined, cut interlining to exact size of cover without turnings. Place it on to wrong side of cover. Fold the turning over it and pin and tack. Clip the scallops at several places to ease the curve into a good shape. (Diagram 1.)

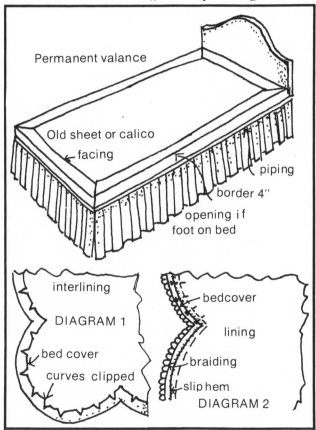

Turn the cover over on to right side. Pin, tack and machine a braid edging about ¼in up from edge.

Turn to wrong side. Cut outer lining to size of bedcover, plus just under ⅓in turnings. Smooth on to interlining, making sure there are no creases. Pin and tack to cover. Clip the curves of this lining, too.

Turn lining in about ⅛in from edge. Slipstitch hem by hand, using a small stitch and matching thread. (Diagram 2.)

This tailored bedspread dominates the decorating theme of the bedroom.

Fitted Divan Cover

covers made like cushions in self or contrasting material. Finish with a slide fastener and pipe the edges.

If the cover is to go over bedclothes, allow 2in extra all round, as well as turnings, or the finished cover will not fit. But if it is to be used in a sitting room and not on a bed, take measurements of divan plus turnings only.

A divan that doubles as a bed should have pillow

Measurements over bedclothes
Width: 3ft, plus 1in turning (½in each side), plus 2in allowance = 3ft 3in.
Length: 6ft 2in, plus 1in turning, plus 2in allowance = 6ft 5in.
Depth: 1ft 8in, plus 1in turning on border, plus ½in top of flounce and 1½in hem, plus 2in allowance = 2ft 1in.

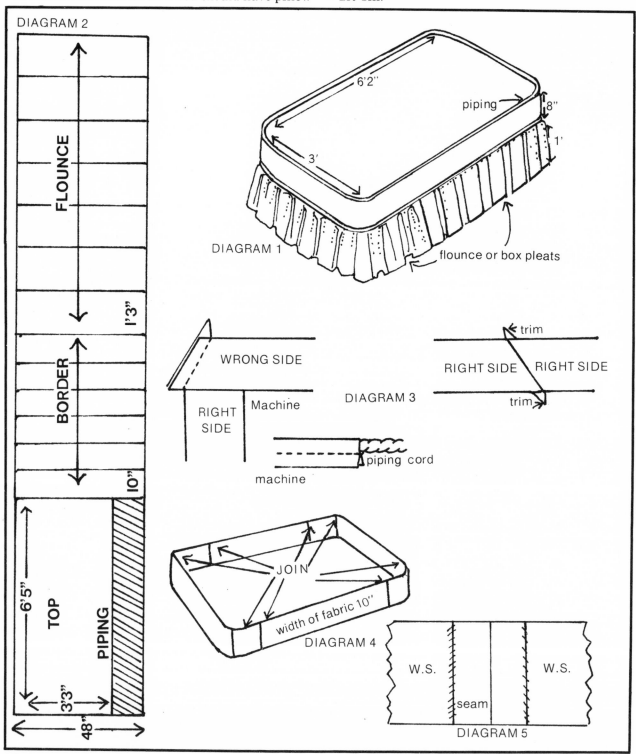

DIAGRAM 2

FLOUNCE

1'3"

BORDER

10"

6'5"   TOP

PIPING

3'3"

48"

piping

6'2"

3'

8"

1'

DIAGRAM 1

flounce or box pleats

WRONG SIDE

RIGHT SIDE   Machine

DIAGRAM 3

machine

piping cord

trim

RIGHT SIDE   RIGHT SIDE

trim

JOIN

width of fabric 10"

DIAGRAM 4

W.S.

seam

W.S.

DIAGRAM 5

FITTED DIVAN COVER (A)

Attractive runners enhance elegant furniture in any room of the house and protect the polished wood of tables and sideboards from being scratched by anything placed upon them.
Brightly-coloured table mats can be made easily and quickly, with little expenditure.

Give an air of individuality to an item by adding a touch of trimming. Fringe is an edge trim made from the threads of the fabric or from yarn; braid is a woven novelty trim finished on both edges.

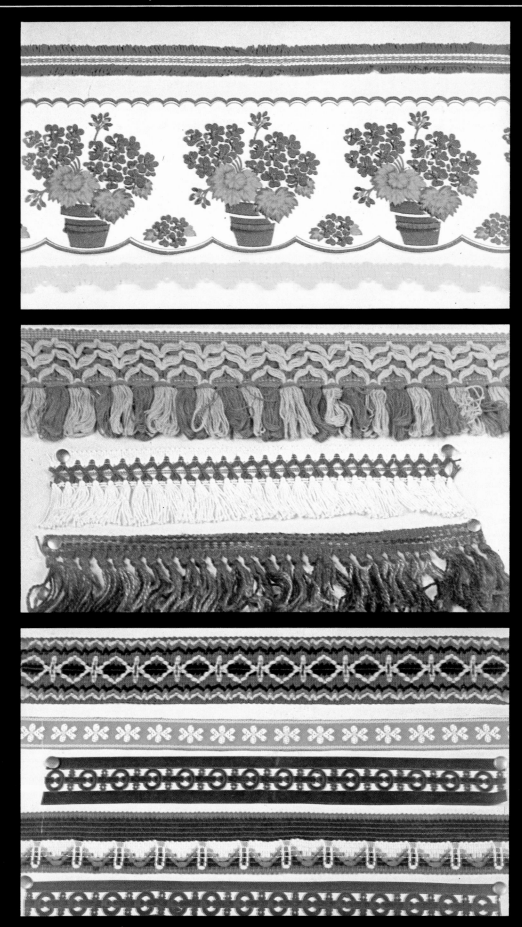

Materials

About 6¾ yards of 48in or 50in furnishing fabric for a standard divan, allowing for bedclothes, or 6⅝ yards without bedclothes. (The yardage includes flounce, allowing one and a half times round divan; or box pleats, three times round. Pillow covers and cushions are extra.) About 14 yards No. 3 or 4 piping cord, shrunk in water and well dried before use.

Step 1: Measure your divan. Diagram 1 shows standard size, but beds differ.

Step 2: If you are unused to cutting out from given measurements, using tailor's chalk and a ruler, make a paper pattern. Then corrections can be made before cutting.

Place pattern on fabric and cut out.

Step 3: Cut 1½in crossway strips on the true cross for covering piping cord. Join to form one long strip. Tack fabric round cord, then machine, using a cording foot if you have one. A cording foot has only one side and so can get closer to cord for a better finish. (Diagram 3.)

Step 4: Slightly round corners of top of cover to prevent corners poking later. But only slightly, otherwise cover will not fit.

Put covered piping cord on to right side of fabric. Pin and tack and clip piping seam at corners before

machining. Only a very experienced machinist can keep the cord straight without tacking it beforehand.

Step 5: Seam border together, arranging joins in same position on each section. (Diagram 4.)

Step 6: Overcast seams and press open. (Diagram 5.)

Step 7: Pin, tack and machine border to piped top of divan cover, right side to right side. Use a cording foot here, too. (Diagram 6.)

Step 8: Turn border over to right side. Pipe lower edge of border also. (Diagram 7.)

Step 9: Flounce or box pleats. Seam as for border. Turn up hem 1in and ½in under. Pin, tack. Machine or slipstitch hem by hand; press hem and seams. (Diagram 8.)

Gather flounce by hand in sections, since this is easier than doing it all at once. For box or inverted pleats, pin and tack into place. A double divan could have 4in box pleats and a 4in space. Try to arrange pleats in same position at each corner.

When pinned and tacked, machine pleats along top to hold them in place. They will be much easier to fix to the border afterwards.

Step 10: Pin pleating or flounce to border, right side to right side. Equalize gathers in flounce. Tack

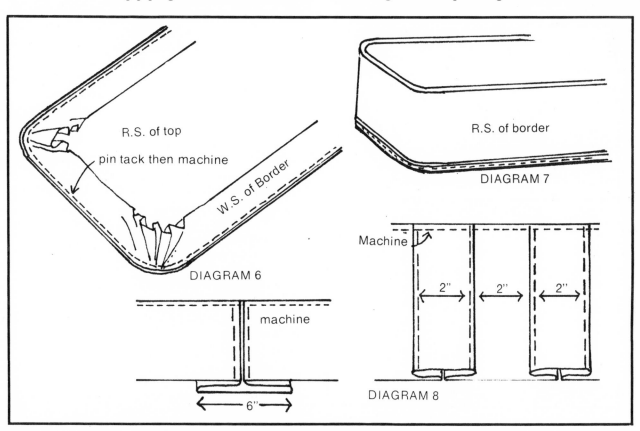

R.S. of top

pin tack then machine

W.S. of Border

DIAGRAM 6

machine

← 6" →

R.S. of border

DIAGRAM 7

Machine

2" 2" 2"

DIAGRAM 8

(B)

and machine. Overcast raw edges. Press well, fold flounce or pleats over to right side.

Overcast inside edges of top of border, piping and any other seams to prevent fraying.

Tailored Box Bedspread

The tailored box bedspread is best for beds with box springs and without footboards. Choose a fabric that does not crease readily.

There are three parts to the spread. The surface fabric to fit the top with ¾in turning all round; the border or boxing strip (either one long strip to go right around the mattress, or two or four strips joined at the bed corners with ¾in turnings allowed at top and bottom); the pleated flounce or skirt with 2in allowed for top turnings and hem.

To measure
For yardage, measure the made-up bed in width, length and depth of the box part, and then measure the skirt allowing extra material for pleats. Make sufficient piping in the bedspread material to do all the seams.

To make
Step 1: Cut the fabric for the top of the bed and join if necessary to cover the full width. Never join a bedspread in the middle, join it twice with narrow strips on either side of the wide centre strip.

Step 2: Join boxing pieces to make one long strip. Then, inserting the piping as you go, pin and sew this strip to the top of the spread. Round the corners slightly when placing the piping in the seam.

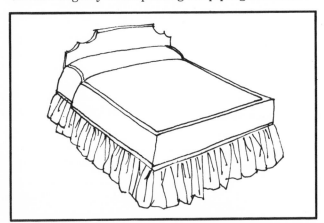

BOXED SPREAD WITH FRILL ATTACHED

Step 3: Join the skirt pieces and turn the hem all the way around. Lay out the pleats, press, and stitch them across the top to hold them in place. Make sure the inner sections of pleats fall at the corners of the bed and that any joins in the skirt are hidden in the pleats.

Step 4: Tack the piping to the lower edge of the boxing then lay this corded edge over the pleats and stitch along the base of the piping through the top of the pleats. Make sure your hem clears the floor by about ½in.

Daisy Bedspread for a Teenager

The latest leather-look fabrics are practical and durable. They can be dry-cleaned and a damp cloth will wipe off most spots and marks. The fabric is soft and supple, easy to sew, drapes well and resists dirt and creases. It is cotton-backed, cuts easily and can be pressed on the WRONG side.

The range of colours includes white and black. Fabric is available in 54in widths and two weights—light and heavy.

Always cut the leather-look fabric in the one direction, either with the right side face up on all pieces or all pieces face down.

Use a long stitch on your machine, about 8 stitches to the inch, a heavy-duty needle and heavy-duty thread.

Use a steam iron to press seams and press only the back of the fabric. Use moderate heat. Never allow the metal face of the iron to come in contact with the face of the fabric.

To measure
For the simple throw-over daisy bedcover shown in the illustration on page 147 take the fabric measurements over the fully-made bed.

Start at the headboard and measure full length of bed and down to the floor at foot. Add about 26in to this the measurement around the pillow.

This is the total length of the finished spread. Get the width by measuring from the floor on one side up and over the bed and down to the floor on other side.

This daisy patterned bedspread would delight any teenager.

Add about two inches for hems to all measurements.

To make the plain spread, you will need about 5½ yards of the leather-look fabric.

To make

Step 1: Cut the fabric into two equal lengths. Place one panel down the centre of the bed. Split the other lengthwise for the two sides. This way you do not have a seam in the centre of the bedspread.

Step 2: Join the side pieces to the centre panel piece with selvage edges together. Pin together before stitching. Clip selvages at intervals.

Step 3: Turn up hems and press.

Daisy decoration

Use felt in bright colours for the daisies. Felt is available in 10in squares or by the yard. It does not fray so saves time in hemming.

Use a dinner plate to cut the circle for the petals and a cup to make the scallops. Outline with pencil and cut out the shapes.

Use a bread and butter plate to cut felt circles for centres.

Cut leaf shapes from felt and straight pieces for stems. Place the centres on the petal pieces and applique or glue to bedspread. Add stem and leaves.

Place daisies so that the top petals come just below edge of the bed on each side.

Round Bolster to hold Divan Pillowcases

To make

Step 1: Roll up your pillows to a sausage shape and tie loosely with string in two places. Measure the overall length and allow 1in for turnings; measure the circumference round the pillows and allow 2in for a lapover, the pillows are inserted in the bolster through the side.

Step 2: Measure the circumference of the end. An easy way is to stand the roll on a dinner plate,

or one that is nearest in size, allow ¾in clearance. Use this plate as the pattern for the ends and cut two circles of fabric and two circles of non-woven interlining. Tack the one piece of fabric to one piece of lining, these make the ends of the bolster.

Step 3: Cut one piece of fabric the length of the pillows (A) and the circumference round the pillows plus the overlap (B).

Step 4: Cut a piece of non-woven interlining.

Step 5: Lay the fabric and lining back to back. Stitch along the sides lengthwise, turn fabric to right side and press flat. Stitch along the ends on the right side to hold them flat.

Step 6: Make two lengths of piping to go round the circumference of the ends. Tack carefully round the two circles slashing the back of the piping where necessary to make a smooth curve.

Step 7: Lay the edge of the long lined piece of fabric to the round circle, overlapping the open ends by 1in. Tack the circle to the fabric piece, check that the pieces fit well then stitch firmly in position.

Step 8: Repeat with the second circle and make sure that the overlap faces the same direction as the first one. Insert pillows in the bolster through the lapover opening.

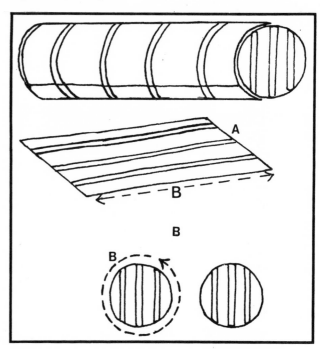

ROUND BOLSTER TO HOLD DIVAN PILLOWS

Boxed Pillowcases

Boxed pillowcases
Matching boxed pillowcases give the finishing touch to your new bedspread.

To make
Step 1: Measure the two pillows end to end, then the width. Cut two rectangles of fabric to the required size, allowing 1in turnings all around. Cut a strip of fabric, 5in wide, to go around the case edges. Allow ½in for joins in the strip.

Step 2: Cut four strips of non-woven interlining for stiffening; two measuring the length of the pillows by 4in wide, the other two the width of the pillows by 4in wide. Sew this lining to inside of box border.

Step 3: Make piping and insert between top of pillowcase and border as you join them. Sew piping around lower box border. Stitch bottom of pillowcase to piped border leaving one end open. Hem this opening and add fasteners.

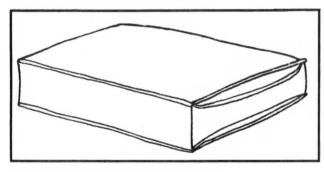

BOXED PILLOWCASES

Bedhead Slipcover and Matching Throwover Quilt

Make a pretty slipcover to decorate the headboard of your bed. As they are loose covers, they are easily taken off and on for laundering or dry cleaning.

To make
Step 1: Cut a paper pattern to the exact shape of the woodwork. Place pattern on fabric and cut out, leaving ½in seams. If headboard is too wide for the fabric, place one length in the centre and split another length for the two sides, matching fabric motifs.

Step 2: Trim selvages off, stitch seams and press.

Step 3: Using the paper pattern, cut a second piece for the back. Cut a long, narrow strip of fabric to go round the headboard on top and sides. This is the boxing strip. With right sides facing join the boxing strip (with piping) to the front cover and to the back, leaving the bottom edge open to slip over the bedhead.

Step 4: Hem the bottom edge.

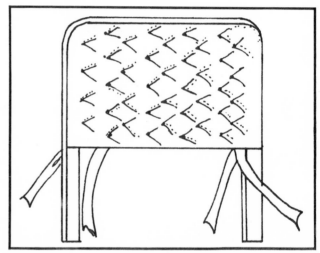

LOOSE COVER FOR A BEDHEAD

A matching throwover quilt
This is quite simple to make and a versatile item to have.

Step 1: For yardage, start at the headboard and measure the full length of the bed down to the floor at the foot. Add measurement around the pillow which is usually 36in. For the width, measure from floor on one side, over the bed and to the floor on the other. Add 2in to each side and ends for hems.

Step 2: Usually two lengths of 50-54in fabric will make this spread for a double bed. Place one length down the centre of the bed. Split the other lengthwise down the centre for the sides. Join the three panel pieces. Pin and stitch. Clip the selvage at intervals. Turn up hem.

Step 3: Add fringe or braid as desired.

To achieve a high standard of quilting the materials must be carefully chosen and
the design and stitchery well planned.

Decorative Bedheads

There are several ways of using fabric as decoration for headboards. For divans (box springs and mattresses) without footboards a framework of wood is needed. This is padded with cottonwool or plastic foam, covered with muslin, then with the decorative fabric.

For the wooden headboard of a regular bedstead, a slipcover may be made or the headboard padded and covered with fabric. If headboard is too wide for width of fabric you are using to cover it, place one length in centre, split another length for the two sides, matching fabric motifs at joins. Cut the selvages off so that the seam will not pull. Stitch these seams and press open.

Irish linen tea towels with floral motifs make attractive coverings for headboards.

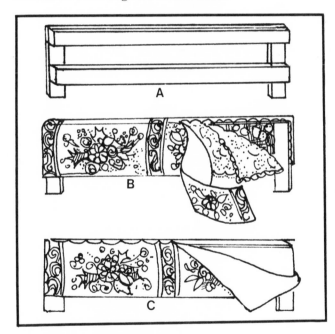

MAKING A HEADBOARD

Divan headboard

Step 1: Make the framework for the headboard of timber 4in or 6in wide and ½in thick. Cut two upright pieces at the required height and two crosswise pieces for the width of the bed. Nail boards together with sturdy nails long enough to clinch on the underside (diag A).

Step 2: Cover the top with a thin strip of moulding. Cut a piece of strong muslin or drill to cover back from side to side and over edge of crosspieces.

Step 3: Tack at intervals, turn to front and stuff space between crossbars with crumpled newspaper. Cover whole front surface with cotton padding or plastic foam (diag B). Lay muslin over this and stretch evenly, using thumbtacks for holding during the stretching. Then tack in place along the edges.

Step 4: Place fabric over front and stretch. Thumbtack in place. Tack in position all around.

The ends and top edges of the headboard may be covered with a simple strip of fabric 3in wide, cut on the cross and long enough to extend up one side, across the top and down the other side (diag C). Fold fabric in half lengthwise and press. Fold raw edges under ½in and press. Lay along headboard with creased line close to back edge. Tack this band in place all along top and sides covering all raw edges of underneath fabric.

Padded headboard

Step 1: Cut a paper pattern to the exact shape of the woodwork. Place fabric on pattern, pin all around. Cut fabric to fit exactly. Get exact centre of fabric by folding lengthwise through centre.

Use plastic foam for padding out to headboard shape and glue to headboard.

Step 2: Place at exact centre of headboard. Smooth out towards side so that no wrinkles or bulges can form.

Step 3: Tack all along wood edge, covering with matching or harmonizing upholsterer's braid. Use upholstery nails and, if necessary, fabric glue under the braid for secure application.

If fabric used for covering is to be quilted or decorated with machine stitching, do this before cutting from pattern.

Frilled Bedcover and Matching Pillowslips

Frilled bedcover and matching pillowslips

This floral bedcover with matching pillowslips is an elegant way to decorate a bedroom. Once you have made the bedspread you can build the colour scheme of the room around it.

You will need 14 yards of 36in or 48in fabric (approximately) for a standard double bed (108in by 90in).

To measure
Take the measurements of the bed you wish to cover with the bed fully made up with sheets and blankets. Allow 2in extra all round as well as the turnings so that the finished cover will fit smoothly.

Measure the top width of the bed, add 1in turning (½in each side) plus 2in allowance. Measure the length from top to foot of bed (about 6ft 2in) plus 1in turnings, plus 2in allowance. Measure from top edge of the bed to the floor, plus ½in top of flounce and 1½in hem.

Material 48in or 50in wide is most economical to use. It is wide enough to cover the top of the bed without seaming and the frill can be made from split widths of the fabric.

The yardage needed will be the length of the top plus the flounce. Allow 1½ times the length round the bed for fullness. Add 2 yards for each frilled pillow. You will also need enough piping cord to go round the top of the bedspread.

To make
Step 1: Cut off a length of fabric long enough to cover the top of the bed plus turnings. Cut the length needed for the flounce and split it down the centre. Cut off the length required for the frilled pillows.

Step 2: Hem the top edge of the bedcover with ½in hem. Join lengths together for flounce and hem bottom edge. Cut 1½in strips on the true bias for covering the piping cord. Join to form one long strip.

Step 3: Tack fabric around the cord, then machine,

using a cording foot if you have one. A cording foot has only one side and so gets closer to the cord for a better finish.

Step 4: Slightly round the corners of the top of the cover to prevent the corners poking later. Sew piping cord to right side of fabric as in diagram. Pin, tack and clip piping seams at corner before machining.

Step 5: Gather the flounce by hand in sections for easy handling. Pin flounce to the top of the bed-cover, right side to right side. Equalize the gathers in the flounce. Tack and machine. Press well, fold flounce to the right side. Overcast inside edges of top, piping and other seams to prevent fraying (see diagram).

Frilled pillowslip

First cut off a 3in strip from each selvage for the pillowslip frill. Cut one piece of fabric 36in by 18in and another 30in by 18in for the main part of the pillowslip.

To make
Step 1: Join the short ends of the two three inch strips to make one long circular piece and gather it to fit round the edges of the 30in by 18in piece. With right sides facing and raw edges level tack them together.

Step 2: Place the 36in by 18in piece on top, right sides facing, so that the three sides are level.

Step 3: To form the tuck-in turn back the extending piece level with the fourth side. This will be the open end of the pillowslip. With the frill inside tack and stitch down the two long sides and across the other end. Turn right side out and press.

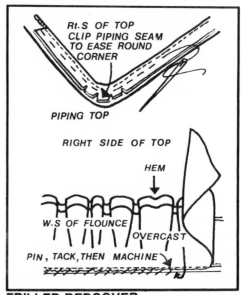

**FRILLED BEDCOVER
AND MATCHING PILLOW SLIPS**

A frilled skirt adds a dainty touch to a bedspread.

A frilled bedcover and matching pillowslips.

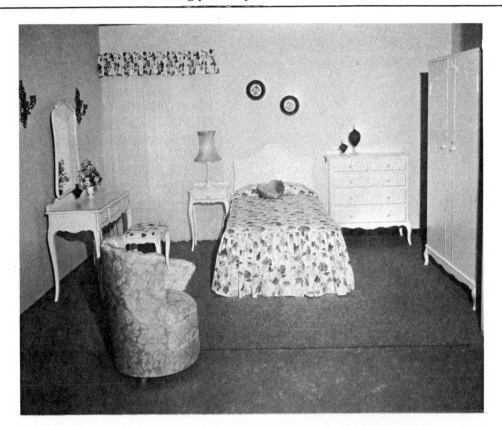

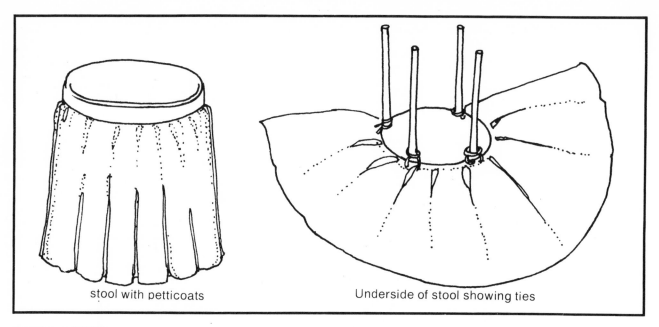

stool with petticoats   Underside of stool showing ties

STOOL COVER

A Stool cover with Full Length Frill

A very cheap way of adding a gay touch to a bedroom is to dress up a stool with a frill or 'drapery'. Some good materials are glazed chintz, small-patterned cretonnes, sprigged dress cotton and organdie flounces.

To make

Step 1: Cut the material on the stool as if you were making a loose cover, make a rectangle or circle to fit the top allowing ½in turnings. Make a border or boxing strip to go round the stool and the depth of the seat and enough piping to cover the fabric joins.

Step 2: Cut a strip of non-woven interlining the same size as the border to stiffen a lightweight fabric. Join border to top circle or rectangle.

Step 3: Measure the depth of frill from the bottom of the seat cushion to within ½in of floor. Allow 1in hem and ½in turnings. Measure the circumference of stool and add half of this measurement for fullness.

Step 4: Cut fabric to these measurements of length and depth and turn up the skirt hem.

Step 5: Gather the top to fit the base of the border and join together inserting piping as you sew. Join side seam of skirt on the wrong side.

Step 6: Make four long ties from folded material and sew by hand to inside of the border at points near legs of stool.

Step 7: Slip cover over stool and tie the material tapes diagonally across the bottom of the underside of the stool or, if suitable, tie round the legs of the stool.

Dressing-table Cover

A pretty dressing table cover will give a new lease of life to a chest of drawers or a dressing table that has seen better days. Any old shabby table can be turned into a graceful piece of bedroom furniture by providing it with frilled 'petticoats'.

If the top of the dressing table is narrow it will be necessary to fit a new and larger top so that it overhangs the underframe and drawers by at least 2in. This will make for easier opening and closing of the drawers which will then not become tangled with the top valance each time they are in use. The valance is attached to the edge of the top while the skirt is hung either on curtain rails fixed to the overhang or fixed to two hinged arms which open out to expose the drawers. You will need to fix either of these attachments to your new top.

If the table is without drawers and there is no

DRESSING TABLE COVER

need to move the curtains then a plastic coated spring wire is all that is needed. Attach this wire with a hook to one side of the dressing table and extend it right round to the other side where it is held firmly with another small hook.

For the curtains themselves any light sheer is suitable if you like a soft feminine look. Taffetas, chintz, spotted muslin and fine cottons are also suitable.

To make

Step 1: Measure the depth from floor to table top allowing 3in for hems and turnings. For fullness measure round the dressing table and allow twice the width for cottons and the like and three times the width if using a sheer fabric. Make the curtains to overlap in the centre. The curtain hems should just clear the floor by about ½in.

Step 2: Make a paper pattern of the top of the dressing table, cut out fabric, and allow ½in turnings all round.

Step 3: Make a pelmet either straight, curved or scalloped or trimmed with a bobble fringe, about 4in deep. Stitch this to a piece of non-woven interlining cut to the same shape. Sew pelmet to top. Interlining will make your top cover washable.

Step 4: Make up the skirt as you would a pair of

unlined simple curtains hemmed at top and bottom and along the sides.

If using a curtain wire make a slot case at the top to take the wire.

If using a curtain rail use either pleater tape and hooks or gathering tapes with hooks that fit into runners on the curtain rail.

If using hinged wooden arms make the top for the dressing table separately and fix fabric down over the edge holding position with drawing pins.

Step 5: Make the valance or pelmet and skirt in four separate pieces. Fix the two front pieces to the hinged wooden arms and the other two pelmets and skirts at either end of the dressing table.

Made this way you will be able to swing the front curtains apart to use the drawers without becoming tangled in an overhanging valance or pelmet.

Your dressing table cover must be kept fresh and neat so make it in such a way that it comes apart easily for laundering.

Tablecloths and other Household Linen

Gay and hard-wearing cloths may be made simply at home from gingham or seersucker, or a lace-trimmed cloth for informal occasions can be made from crocheted lace or coarse bought lace. While good linen on which fine work can be done should be used to make an embroidered tea cloth which may well become a treasured possession in your household. Many kinds of embroidery can be used to decorate a plain cloth and edgings or trims can also be added to make pretty cloths.

Table napkins can be made to match the table-cloth and should be approximately 17 inches square when finished. However, the size may vary to suit your individual requirements.

Table mats may be round, square or oblong in shape and can be made in a variety of materials. Of course the material should be washable. Circular mats for example can be finished around the edges with scalloping or edged with braid or bound with a contrasting bias binding. Embroidered designs can be added in the centre or at the corners to add a pretty touch to plain materials, or motifs can be appliqued onto the material. There are many decorative variations which are easy to work but which can completely change the appearance of a table setting.

Circular Tablecloths

Circular tablecloths can be used for a dinner party or to cover an otherwise worn and shabby table permanently.

The round tablecloth may be short or floor length. If floor length it should clear the floor by an inch.

The cloth can be made from any width of fabric, a sheet is ideal for a floor length cloth since it does not need joining; 54in fabric is suitable for the shorter length cloth. Narrower fabric means joins.

To measure
The amount of fabric needed depends on the size of the table and the width of fabric to be used. To find the amount needed for a floor length cloth measure from the floor to the edge of the table, across the top diameter then to the floor again on the other side. If the measurement is wider than the fabric width you will need twice the amount of fabric.

The diameter of the cloth multiplied by 3½ times will give the amount of braid or fringe needed to trim the hem of the cloth. The same amount of bias binding will be needed for neatening the hem.

For a simple circular cloth you will need 1½ yards 54in fabric and 8 yards trimming.

To make
Step 1: Mark off a circle on the 54in fabric using your tape measure or a piece of string. Push a drawing pin into the 27in mark of your tape measure and secure the tape with the drawing pin at exact centre of the fabric. Hold a tailor's chalk or pencil at end of the tape measure and carefully draw the circle with the tape held taut (diag 1). Cut out the circle, hem and trim as desired.

To make the cloth when fabric is not wide enough to avoid joins cut the fabric in half across the width to give two pieces of equal length. Avoid a centre seam by cutting the second length in half lengthways and joining one to each side of the main piece.

Step 2: Fold the fabric into four and make a compass from a piece of string and a pencil or piece of chalk. Pin the string to the top corner and draw an arc with the pencil making the radius half that of the diameter of the floor length cloth. Cut along this marked line through four thicknesses. Cut one at a time so that they are accurate (diag. 2).

Step 3: Open out your large circle of fabric and neaten the hem by stitching the opened edge of the bias binding to the outside of the cloth ½in from the edge. Trim and turn binding to the wrong side and machine the other turned edge of binding to the cloth.

Step 4: Pin and tack the fringe or braid to the outside hem.

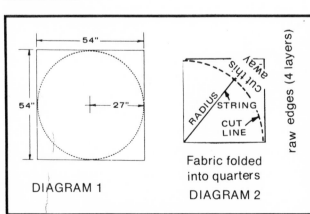

CIRCULAR TABLECLOTH

PatioCloth

Here is a cloth which you can make in half an hour, even if you are a beginner, for it is all straight sewing. Choose a gay colour to brighten your table or a pattern to tone with your china. Either way it will give a new look to your party theme.

You will need 2 yards of 50-54in colourful cotton fabric and 12 yards of heavy white jumbo rickrack braid.

To make
Step 1: Hem the two cut ends and your basic cloth is ready for trimming.

Step 2: Stitch 7 yards of the rickrack braid round the edge of the cloth.

Step 3: Stitch another row of white rickrack 12in from all sides forming a rectangle on the centre part of the cloth.

Your cloth is ready to put on the table.

Table napkins
Make table napkins by cutting 18in squares from contrasting material and hemming or fringing the edges.

Add a glittering centrepiece and candles for a touch of glamour.

This round cloth with matching napkins makes a pretty luncheon set.

Place Mats

Place mats are a simple and effective way of brightening up a table. They are quick and easy to make and almost any type of fabric may be used.

Material
Choose fabrics that are colourfast and washable: remember they will spend a lot of time in and out of the washtub.

Choose fabrics that are suitable to the occasion. Heavy burlaps and coarse linens are suitable for outdoor patio lunches, pretty cottons and linens for lunches, and dainty mats with appliques and lacy trims for informal dinners.

1 yard of 36in fabric will make six place mats each 18in long and 12in wide.

To make
Step 1: Cut the fabric to size then hem the edges or fringe them by drawing threads till you have the required depth of fringe on each side.

Step 2: Trim with washable, colourfast decorative braids or fringes. Add appliques, pockets for cutlery if they are to be used outdoors. Use textile paint and add your own motifs or embroider them in the colours of your choice.

Lace trims and insertions give a more formal trim and are easy to sew to the edges.

Table napkins
So set a pretty table any time with a new set of place mats and matching napkins. One yard of fabric will make nine napkins each 12in square. For a co-ordinated look, trim them to match your place mats.

To make

Step 1: Straighten the two cut edges of the cloth. Use a 9in plate and a 6in saucer for tracing the scrolls on the cloth. Hem the cloth and trim with the white lace.

Step 2: Use the plate and saucer to make scrolls at the corners as desired (diag 1).

Step 3: Trace the scroll design in the centre of the cloth as shown (diag 2) and outline with the white lace.

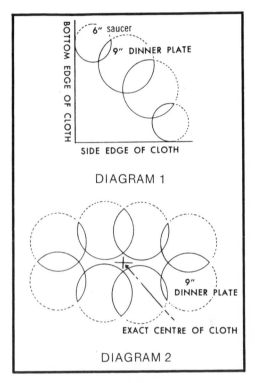

DIAGRAM 1

DIAGRAM 2

LACE SCROLL CLOTH

Lace Scroll Cloth

A pretty cloth to make for a luncheon.

Material
It requires 2 yards of 54in plain cotton fabric and 15 yards of narrow white cotton lace to trim the edges of the cloth and to make the motif in the centre.

Barbecue Runner

Summer days mean outdoor meals and barbecues. Add to the fun of your next barbecue with this gay and ornamental cloth and runner.

Material

For the basic tablecloth you will need 2 yards of 54in cotton fabric. Make a narrow ½in hem all round the cloth and machine.

For the runner you will need ⅔ yard 54in fabric, or 1 yard 36in fabric. Be sure to use colour-fast fabrics for cloth and appliques.

If using 54in fabric, cut in half crosswise into two 12in x 54in strips. Cut 18in off each strip to give two 12in x 36in pieces.

Use the two 12in x 18in pieces left over for napkins.

If using 36in fabric, cut crosswise into three 12in x 36in strips. Set one strip aside for napkins. Join two 12in x 36in strips with a ¼in seam to make a runner 12in x 71½in.

For the barbecue appliques you will need 1 yard of 36in beige fabric; 1 piece white fabric 4in x 12in; 4⅝ yards white rickrack braid (jumbo size); ¾ yard gold rickrack (regular); ½ yard red rickrack (regular); 1½ yards brown rickrack (regular); ⅓ yard green baby rickrack; 1¾ yards 1¼in wide red tape; ½ yard 1¼in white tape; ⅜ yard 1¼in green tape.

To make

Step 1: Put a ¼in hem around the runner. Stitch the white jumbo rickrack braid over the edges on the right side, catching just the points of the rickrack.

Step 2: Copy the applique pattern pieces from the diagram (below) on to tissue paper, enlarging to required size. Follow cutting directions on pattern pieces.

Step 3: Stitch ⅛in inside all edges of pieces cut from fabric. Turn and baste edges, clipping at curves.

Step 4: Sew rickrack braid on mustard jar and sauce label as indicated on the pattern pieces.

Step 5: Divide each half of the runner into thirds by placing basting lines every 12in. Place indivi-

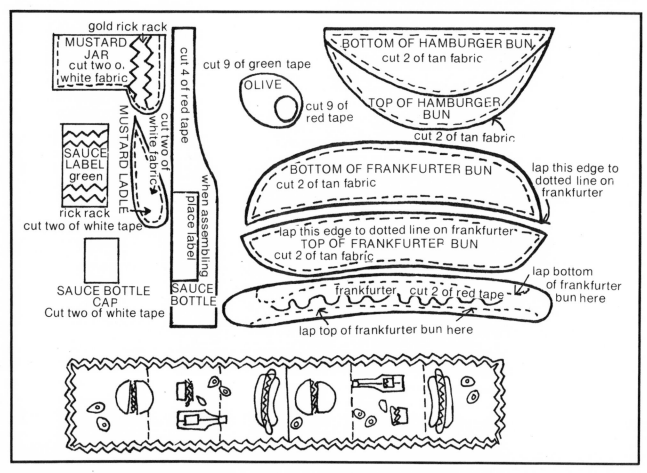

BARBECUE TABLERUNNER

dual motifs on runner as indicated in bottom diagram.

Step 6: Applique olives, sauce bottle and frankfurter motifs to runner.

Step 7: Hand applique mustard jar and ladle, frankfurter buns in place (lap bun sections over frankfurters as shown on pattern pieces, slipping a piece of gold rickrack under top bun).

Step 8: For the hamburger, applique lower bun section in place. Sew three lines of brown rickrack above this to represent meat, and a line of red rickrack to represent sauce. Lap top bun section halfway over red rickrack, and applique in place.

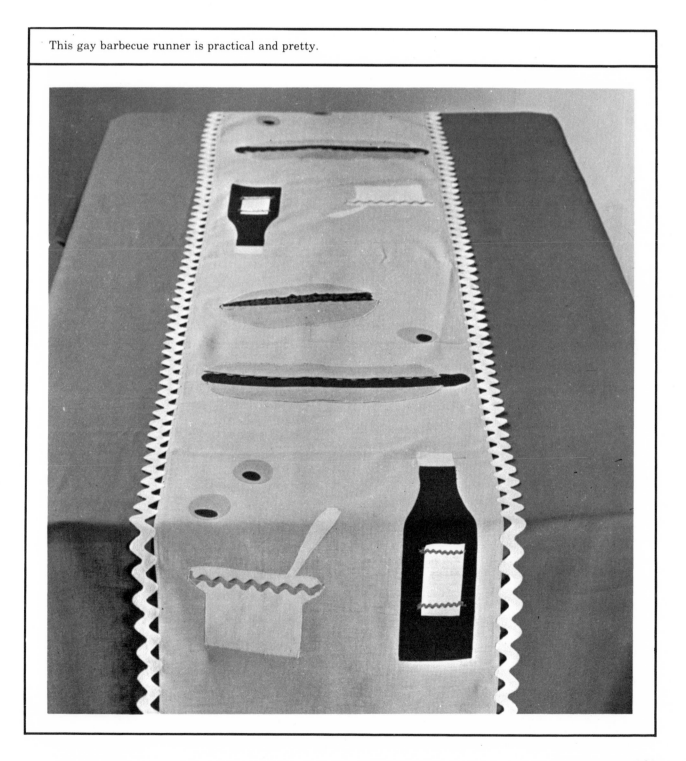

This gay barbecue runner is practical and pretty.

A patio cloth for informal entertaining.

This lace scroll design is pretty for a luncheon cloth.

Place mats are a simple way to brighten up a table.

A pretty table can be set anytime with place mats and matching napkins.

Decorative Accessories

Most of us from time to time have leftover materials we have used in dressmaking, curtain-making or furniture renovation. Keep all your scraps of materials and when there are enough to be used make them into an attractive patchwork article or use them for making cushions.

A room without cushions looks quite bare but good cushions are expensive although fairly easy to make. Some new scatter cushions can make a lot of difference to a room where maybe you are not planning a big renovation of the furnishings.

Chunky Floor Cushions

Chunky foam-filled cushions are handy for extra seating when you suddenly have a housefull of guests and not enough chairs. As well the cushions can add bright decorative touches to a room.

Materials
To make the vinyl chunky cushion pictured you will need a 20in square piece of foam plastic or rubber 12in thick; two 27in slide fasteners; 1¾ yards of 54in vinyl; matching linen or Terylene thread for sewing.

If you are unable to buy foam 12in thick, buy several thinner pieces in the required size and glue together with fabric adhesive.

When sewing vinyl use the linen or Terylene thread and a large stitch on your sewing machine.

A mixture of equal parts of glycerine and water rubbed along the seam will prevent your machine from sticking to the vinyl.

To make
Step 1: From the vinyl cut two 20in squares allowing ¾in seams.

Step 2: Then cut two strips, each 13in wide and 44in long. Join them together along the narrow edges to form a circle. This is the boxing strip for the sides. Allow 2″ seams.

Step 3: Sew one long side all round the top of the cushion cover, right sides facing and raw edges level. Make sure the seams in the boxing come at the corners of the cushion.

Step 4: Join the other long edge of the boxing to bottom of cushion cover along one side only. Turn to right side.

Step 5: Starting from the corners formed by the side stitched to the boxing, insert slide fasteners on three sides so that they meet together in the centre of the side opposite the one stitched to the boxing; they then form a lid-like opening.

Step 6: Insert the foam cushion and pull cover evenly over the foam. Close slide fasteners. Your cushion is complete.

This attractive vinyl covered floor cushion is handy for extra seating.

Six Cushions

Cushions add a note of bright colour to a room and often give the finishing touch to the decor. Piled in colourful profusion they will dress up a feminine bedroom or add a touch of comfort to the living room.

If you are using cushions outdoors, cover them with a fabric that will stand up to the weather. The new plastics are the answer. All you need do is wipe them with a cloth after rain or dew. Use plastic foam, rubber or kapok for filling or the solid foam rubber or plastic cushion shape.

Always make an inner case of unbleached calico to take the filling. If this is made slightly larger than the outer cover you will have a firm cushion. Do not overstuff cushions, as this makes then too hard for comfort; too little filling gives a limp appearance.

A bolster cushion

Material
You will need 1 yard 36in chintz; 1½ yards bobble fringe for trimming; 1 moulded foam rubber or plastic bolster shape. (Size used approx. 25in x 9in diameter.)

To make
Cut one piece of fabric 25in long and 28in wide. Cut 2 circles each 9½in in diameter. Stitch the bobble fringe to the 28in edges on the right side. Turn to wrong side and sew the 25in sides together with a short seam at each end, leave a large opening to insert the bolster shape. Join the circular pieces one to each end of the tube. Turn to right side. Insert bolster pad. Slipstitch opening.

Fringed triangle cushion

Material
You will need ¾ yard 42in furnishing satin; 3¼ yards of cotton fringe; 1 triangular moulded shape in desired size.

To make
Make a pattern by placing the triangular shape on the paper and trace around it. Cut out the pattern allowing one inch more on all sides. Place on the fabric and cut out. Pattern will fit economically if you turn it upside down to cut second triangle.

To make up cushion: Place the two triangular pieces together right sides facing. Stitch together with ½in seams leaving one side partly open to

insert pad. Trim corners and seams. Turn to right side. Insert pad and slipstitch opening by hand. Sew fringe to outer edge by hand. Sew to centre of cushion in triangle design by hand.

Square cushion with padded border

Material
You will need ½ yard 48in fabric; 2 yards piping cord; one 11in square moulded foam rubber or plastic shape. Wadding to pad border.

To make
Cut two 16in squares from the fabric and enough 1½in bias strips to cover cord. Join the strips together into one length and cover the piping cord. Stitch the covered cord to the raw edges of one square. Join ends neatly. With right sides facing stitch the two squares together leaving the two opposite sides unstitched for turning out and inserting the padding. Turn to right side and press well.

Mark a 10in square in the centre of the square. Stitch along three sides of this square leaving one side unstitched. Insert pad. Stitch up the fourth side of this inner square. Stuff the two stitched sides of the border with wadding using a ruler to press it in. Fill the unstitched sides pinning the turned edges as you fill each one up. Slipstitch these edges together invisibly by hand.

Round boxed cushion with quilted top

Material
You will need an 18in square of chintz or other floral cotton with a pattern suitable for quilting; an 18in square of wadding and a piece of calico the same size; 20in of matching or contrasting fabric 36in wide; 3 yards piping cord; 1 round boxed foam rubber or plastic shape 16in diameter.

To make
Quilt the patterned fabric. Place wadding on wrong side of fabric and place calico over it. Tack the three pieces together firmly. With the quilting attachment of your sewing machine follow the outline of printed design on right side of fabric. Remove tacking.

Cut a 16in circle from your quilted fabric. Cut another 16in circle from the plain fabric and a boxing strip 4in wide and 46in long (join if needed).

Cut bias strips 1½in wide, join these to make a strip long enough to cover piping cord.

To make up the cushion: Join the short ends of

Á bolster cushion, a fringed triangle cushion and a square cushion with a padded border.

A frilled cushion, a round boxed cushion, and a flat bordered cushion.

the boxing strip together. Cover piping cord with bias strips by stitching close to cord with cording foot of your machine. Stitch piping to raw edges of boxing strip, both sides. Join quilted top to one piped edge of boxing strip. Join bottom circle of plain fabric to other edge of boxing strip leaving an opening large enough to insert pad. Insert pad and slipstitch opening.

Flat bordered cushion

Material
You will need ½ yard 36in striped cotton; 1½ yards black bobble fringe; one inset pad 12in diameter.

To make
Cut two 18in circles from the striped fabric. Stitch bobble fringe to the right side of one circle. With right sides facing stitch the two circles together leaving about 12in unsewn. Turn to right side and press well. Mark in centre of cover with pencil or chalk an 11½in circle. Stitch on this marked line leaving about one-third open to insert pad. Slip pad inside this circular piece, pin and sew round remainder of circle. Slipstitch opening.

Frilled cushion

Material
You will need ¾ yard 36in fabric; 2 buttons ⅝in diameter; an inner pad 12in diameter.

To make
Cut two circles from the fabric 12½in diameter and three 4in wide strips across the width of fabric for frill.

Join the four inch strips together across the short ends, form a tiny hem along one edge. Make circle. Run two rows of large, loose machine stitching along the other edge for gathering the frill.

Pull up gathering and pin to the outside edge of one circular piece. Distribute gathers evenly. Stitch frill around circle. Join the second circle leaving an opening to insert centrepad. Slipstitch opening. Cover button with fabric. Stitch through centre of cushion.

Decorative Quilting

Quilting is not difficult and will give years of warmth and wear. It can turn an ordinary piece of sewing into something that has an heirloom quality. A floral bedspread becomes a thing of beauty if you quilt the floral motifs on it, a plain fabric cover looks beautiful with a quilted design on it. Cushions take a new dimension when they are quilted.

Quilting is a method of stitching several thicknesses of material to give a raised effect and for added warmth. It may be done by hand or by sewing machine that has quilting attachments.

The simplest method is to work straight rows of stitching to form squares, rectangles, diamond shapes. Do this quilting before you make up the cushion or other item and trim to size needed.

Materials
For the backing muslin, lawn, calico are suitable. For the interlining use synthetic or cotton wadding as synthetics are washable and fluff up.

The main cover fabric should be lightweight if the article being made is large, otherwise almost any fabric may be used.

For natural fibre fabrics use a mercerised silk thread and for synthetics a nylon thread. If you choose thread two or three shades darker it will emphasize the design.

To make
Cut your fabric to size required for the article to be made and add an extra 1in seam allowance all round to take up any movement when you are sewing the main fabric, interlining and backing together. Make a sandwich of the layers.

Place the main fabric face down on a table with the wrong side up, lay the wadding over this, then the backing. Pin all three layers together.

On the wrong side tack together around outside with long stitches, making sure the main fabric is smooth on top. Work several rows of tacking across the fabric to hold the layers firmly in position.

Stitching by machine: There is a quilting attachment on your machine. Use a sharp needle in a size to suit your fabric, and a long stitch to take in extra thickness.

It is wise to try out your stitching on a piece of fabric first. You may have to lessen the pressure on the needle bar and slacken the tension.

Diamonds: Make two rows of machine stitching diagonally from corner to corner and crossing at the centre. Work outwards on either side of each diagonal line of stitching in parallel rows of machining. Start each row at the same end to prevent undue puckering. Make sure the fabric is lying flat by placing your hands either side of the foot to hold the fabric smooth.

Squares: Machine from the centre of one side to the centre of the other side. Continue machining outwards in parallel lines on either side of this centre line. Repeat the machining across these lines to make squares.

To keep the machining straight use the quilting foot. This has an adjustable bar to guide along the rows and an upturned foot to run smoothly over the padding.

Designs: If the main cover fabric has a floral design, period design stripe or some other design use the motifs as a guide for your stitching. If the fabric is plain draw your design on it with tailor's chalk then stitch along these lines. Tack around the motif on the right side before machining.

Making up: When you have completed quilting your fabric, trim to required size and neaten all edges with machine zig zag stitch or overcast by hand.

If making a throwover bedspread, finish edges with binding, plain bias or self fabric cut on the cross to make the bias.

For cushions sew back cover to quilted fabric with right sides facing.

Leave an opening to turn to right side and fill cushion. Sew up opening by hand.

Trapunto Cushion

Trapunto work used to make raised designs on cushions brings a new dimension in making decorative pieces for the home.

Materials required
You will need a length of satin fabric for the size of the cushion you wish to make, the one we made was 14in square; an equal length of silk organza; a small quantity of cotton wool or synthetic filling for the padding.

To make
Step 1: Cut the cover to the size required then cut the organza to fit.

Step 2: Trace the flower motif centrepiece on to the centre of one layer of organza. You may choose a rose, a daisy or some other simple flower. Mark the petals round the centre and place this traced piece over the centre of one side of the cover.

Step 3: Using a straight machine stitch, sew round the outside of the centre of the flower leaving a 2in opening at one side. Insert a thin layer of padding through the opening, even it out as you do so. Stitch this opening. Fill in the centre with machine stitching to hold the padding.

Step 4: Next stitch along each side of the petals following the traced outline.

Step 5: Leave an opening at the top of each petal, pad the petals and stitch up the opening. Tack a piece of tissue paper or greaseproof paper to the back of the work to prevent stretching during stitching.

Step 6: Attach one of the fancy stitch discs to your machine and work round each petal over the original stitching. If you do not have a machine that does fancy stitches work chain stitch or other embroidery stitches over the outer line of machining for a good finish.

Step 7: Tear the paper away from the back of the work and make up the cushion in the usual way.

A trapunto cushion adds an interesting touch to the decor of any room.

Boxed Chair Seat Cushions (Dining Chairs)

These little cushions will make your dining chair seats more comfortable when you linger over coffee after dinner. Because chair seats vary with different makes, you will need to make a paper pattern of the seat.

Materials

Using your pattern, work out the yardage needed for each chair. Allow ½in seams, 1in wide boxing strips and ties for each cushion. Add fabric yardage together if you are covering several chairs.

Remember, if you are using fabric with a large motif you will need to centre the design on the paper pattern. You must have two motifs for each cushion so that if you turn them over the design will be centred on either side. You will also need piping cord No. 1 size and enough fabric either matching the cushion or plain contrasting fabric to cover the cord. There should be enough piping cord to go round the cushion twice, top and bottom of the boxing strip. Use foam rubber or plastic foam 1in thick and cut to the shape of the chair seat for filling the cushions. And finally a 16in slide fastener for each chair cushion.

To make

Step 1: Press a sheet of white butcher's paper or brown paper over the chair seat and pencil in the outline. Cut out the seat shape.

Step 2: Cut foam pad to shape, making it about ¼in larger than the paper pattern.

Step 3: Lay paper pattern on fabric, centre motifs if using large patterned fabric and cut two fabric pieces, one for the top, the other for the bottom of the cushion, allowing ½in seam allowance on each one. This will make the finished cushions a firm fit.

Step 4: Now cut enough 2in wide strips which, when joined together will go round the cushion. Cut four strips each 2in wide and 16in long for ties. Cut enough 1½in wide bias strips in self or plain fabric to cover the piping cord for each cushion. Allow twice the length round the cushion plus 2in for seams.

Step 5: Make a continuous bias strip to cover cord and stitch it to the edge of top and bottom cushion pieces, finish ends of cord by butting them together.

Step 6: Make the ties, sew long sides together with right sides facing, then turn to right side and press. Stitch a pair of ties to inside back corners of the bottom piece. Join the short ends of the boxing strip to make a circle.

Step 7: Sew one cushion piece to one long edge of the boxing strip, with right sides facing. Slash the curved edges and the back inner corners to make the seam lie flat and without puckers. Stitch the other cushion piece to the other edge of the boxing strip in the same way. Leave the back edge open between the corners to insert the foam filling.

Step 8: Pin and tack the opened slide fastener to the opening and stitch closely to the teeth.

Step 9: Insert the pad, and close slide fastener.

Make the cushions for the rest of your dining chairs in the same way.

Tie to the back of the chair with the ties to hold them in position.

Bean Bag Chairs

For casual comfort and informal occasions, bean bag chairs are ideal.

Materials needed for each 'chair'

Three yards of 54in wide fabric; one 10in slide fastener; heavy-duty thread; eight cubic feet of pelleted Styrene foam filling.

To make

Step 1: Draw a pattern for end A as shown in diagram 1, using 5¾in radius for circle and allowing ¾in beyond fold line.

Step 2: Draw a pattern for B sections as shown in diagram 2, having points A to J the following distances from centre line: A, 3¾in; B, 6½in; C, 7⅞in; D, 8⁹⁄₁₆in; E, 8⅝in; F, 8¼in; G, 7⅜in; H, 5⅝in; J, 2¹¹⁄₁₆in. Cut pattern double for complete section.

Step 3: Cut two A and six B. Cut one complete

circle with an 8in diameter for C (see cutting layout).

Step 4: Stitch two B sections together with a flat-felled seam, making original plain seam ½in from curved edge. Seam third B section to the first two and add other sections in the same manner. Seam first and last B sections together, forming a football-shaped

piece with open ends. Sew circle C to B sections at smaller end (where J is located on diagram).

Step 5: Fold each A section along fold line and place folded edges along centre of slide fastener so they meet; stitch along each side and across ends as shown in diagram 3. Blind-stitch from ends of slide fastener to edge of circle at each side.

Step 6: Open slide fastener slightly and attach A to other end of B sections. Open slide fastener and turn right side out. Fill loosely with Styrene foam filling.

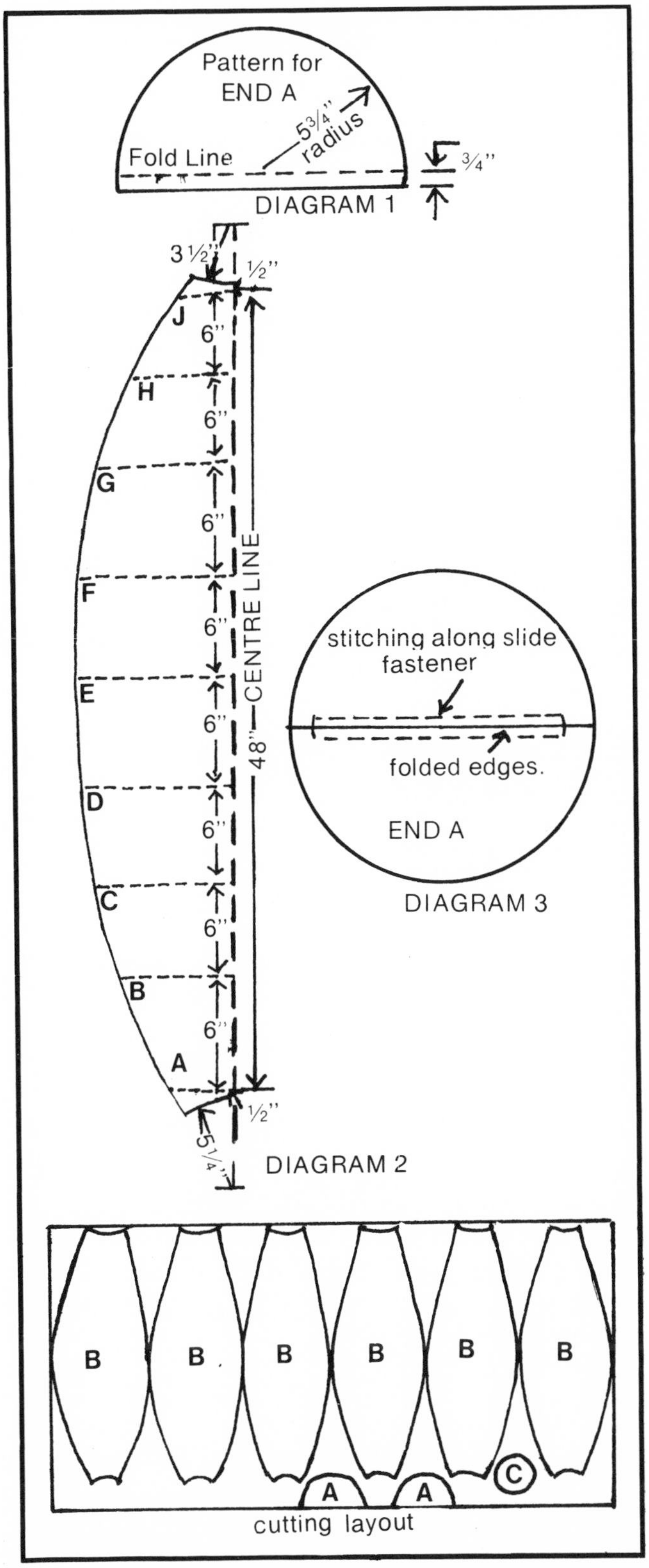

Patchwork

Most people who sew, hoard odds and ends of fabric that are too pretty to throw away and yet not large enough to make anything practical. So if you have numerous pieces of fabrics, closely woven cottons are ideal, why not turn them into a piece of patchwork?

A template
To keep your pieces all the same size you will need a template, which will enable you to cut accurate paper shapes—the basis of all good patchwork. The templates should be cut from a stiff, firm material, otherwise they will lose their shape after a certain amount of use. Very stiff cardboard or thin metal is preferable. The size and shape are entirely a matter of choice, depending on the size of the work you have in mind and the material available.

Templates may be almost any geometric shape, but for the beginner the hexagon is the easiest and most commonly used to make an effective series of patterns in a variety of colours.

Draw on paper a hexagon, each side measuring 2in. Inside this draw a smaller hexagon, each side 1½in. Glue to firm cardboard. Leave to dry.

With a sharp razor blade cut round the inside line of the hexagonal shape to make the window, this enables you to see that your template has been placed on the straight of the fabric. Now cut around the larger outline and the template is complete.

How to cut patches
If you want the larger hexagon patches, the outside edge is the guide for drawing the paper pattern. Add an allowance for turnings when cutting the fabric. For smaller patches use the inside 'window' shape. Cut your papers to this small inside size and your fabric to the outside edge size.

Pattern for END A
Fold Line
5¾" radius
¾"
DIAGRAM 1

3½" ½"
J
6"
H
6"
G
6"
F
6"
48" CENTRE LINE
E
6"
D
6"
C
6"
B
6"
A
½"
5¾"
DIAGRAM 2

stitching along slide fastener
folded edges.
END A
DIAGRAM 3

B B B B B B
A A C
cutting layout

BEAN BAG CHAIR

To make

Step 1: Gather scraps of fabric together, select your colour range, press the chosen scraps and work out your colour scheme.

Step 2: Make the paper pattern, using any firm paper, draw round the outside of your hexagonal template, holding the sharp pencil upright, so that you draw accurately against the edge. (If you slope your pencil you will get a fractional difference in the paper sizes. This makes it impossible to sew the patches up neatly. You can't cheat at patchwork, so take care with this part.)

Step 3: Next, make the fabric shapes, placing the template on the wrong side of the fabric on a hard surface. Through the 'window' you will see when the pattern is nicely centred and straight with the grain or selvage. Now draw round the template with a coloured pencil which shows on your fabric. This will indicate exactly where you should place the paper pattern on your fabric patch. Draw another pencil outline just under half an inch outside the first to give a turning line all round.

Step 4: Cut out the patch round the outer line. Start by cutting your centre patch and the first ring of six patterned patches round it, in your chosen colours.

Step 5: Now place a paper pattern on the wrong side of the fabric patch over the pencilled lines. Hold the pattern flat and turn the surplus edges in a single hem over the paper, being careful to make six neat corners, then tack through paper and fabric, keeping the patch neat and taut.

Step 6: With firm stitches oversew (on the paper sides) one side of the centre patch to one side of a patterned or coloured one. Add the next patterned or coloured patch to the next side edge until all the sides of the centre patch have another patch joined to them.

Step 7: Join up the six radiating seams and you have your patchwork well begun and by now you will see the next step.

Step 8: Make a whole series of these motifs then, when you think you have enough, lay them out on the floor or a broad table and arrange them into a pleasing design.

Step 9: Start joining these large motifs together in the same way as you did the single patches.

Step 10: When you have completed your patchwork to the required size you will need single patches to finish the shape.

Step 11: Add a plain border of fabric as a final finish.

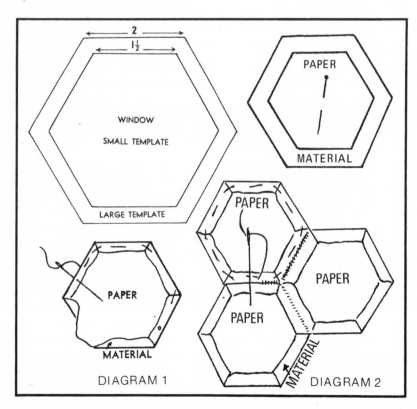

DIAGRAM 1 DIAGRAM 2

PATCHWORK

174

Patchwork is an ideal method of using up odd scraps of material, but care must be taken in arranging the various colours and patterns.

Lampshades

Making your own lampshades saves money. It also means that you can match them to your own soft furnishings, and it is one of the simplest ways of adding bright colour notes to a room.

It is important that the lampshade be in proper proportion to the lamp base. The diameter of the shade can equal the height of the base from table top to the bottom of the shade. The depth of the shade should not be less than one-third and not more than two-thirds the height of the base.

Use pins with care when preparing your shade as pin marks will show when the lamp is illuminated. Secure seams with two rows of stitching. For a good frame use cross stitch in sewing the hood and lining.

A Drum Lampshade

The drum lampshade is quick and easy to make and is a suitable shape to use on almost any style of lamp.

Materials required
Two lampshade rings the same diameter, one plain, the other with a ring in the centre to take the lamp fitting; self adhesive parchment (it has a sticky back) or buckram; covering fabric; clear adhesive, two clothes pegs for clamping, decorative braid for trimming top and or bottom of shade.

Contact or self adhesive parchment is available in sizes 12in high and 48in long at about $2 and 18in high and 48in long about $3.

To make
Step 1: Measure the circumference of the ring with a tape measure, adding ½in for overlap. Next decide the depth of the lampshade. Cut a rectangle of parchment and a rectangle of fabric to these two measurements.

Step 2: Place the wrong side of the fabric to the sticky side of the parchment and iron carefully with a moderately hot dry iron. Turn over and iron again on the back of the parchment. Do not have the iron too hot or the parchment may scorch.

Step 3: Shape into a drum with the fabric side out. Overlap the ends by about ½in and stick with clear adhesive. Use the clothes pegs top and bottom to hold the shape while the adhesive dries. If you do not use adhesive, stitch the join by hand, the pegs will help you to keep the drum shape.

Step 4: Insert rings, top and bottom, with the ring fitting in correct position for use on the lamp. Secure rings to parchment with several oversew stitches.

Step 5: Stick white adhesive tape round the top and bottom folding it over neatly to the wrong side to conceal rings and hold them in place. Snip at struts.

Step 6: Add decorative trims to top and bottom to conceal tape.

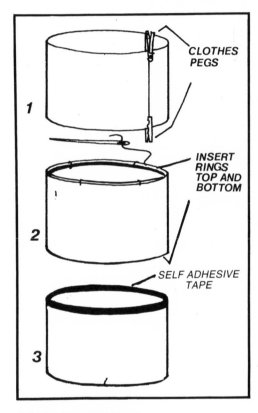

DRUM LAMPSHADE

A Scalloped Lampshade

An attractive lamp with a bright shade will bring colour interest to a room immediately. This lampshade is not hard to make and will save you money. Wire frames can be bought or made to order in any shape or size at most large stores. Frames are painted.

Materials

One waisted frame with scalloped edges in size required (made to order by large stores) (we used one 8in × 12in deep); 1 yard lining 36in wide taffeta or lining satin; 1¼ yards of 36in wide Thai silk, satin or taffeta for cover; tape for binding frame, thread for sewing; 2½ yards gold braid.

To bind frame

Binding the frame is the most important part of lampshade making. It must be tight and even or the shade will be lumpy at the struts. Soft fabrics used to cover it will sag if binding is loose.

Bind all parts of the shade except the wires and ring used to hold the frame to the base. Cover the downward struts then top and bottom edges.

Step 1: Loop about 1in of tape over the top ring of frame, hold this short end firmly against the first strut. Take the long end and start binding it firmly in place. Continue winding the tape diagonally down the strut so that each edge slightly overlaps the last.

Step 2: To make sure the binding is tight give a firm pull after each turn of the tape. Continue to bottom of strut.

Step 3: To finish off take an extra turn round the wire at the bottom and stitch firmly in place. Cut off tape leaving about 1in hanging.

Step 4: Bind all struts the same way leaving about an inch of tape free at the bottom each time.

Step 5: Bind the top ring. When finished stretch tape firmly and stitch in position. Bind the lower ring binding in the loose ends from each strut as you go.

Step 6: When the frame is covered cut off surplus tape, turn edge under and stitch firmly.

To make lining

Step 1: Make a pattern of the shade from brown paper. Place paper over a cushion so that the soft surface takes the shape of the shade, press one side of the frame down on it and outline shape with pencil, taking care to keep scallop shapes.

Step 2: Cut from brown paper allowing ¼in seams. Place pattern on the cross of lining material and cut out. Repeat for other half of lining.

Step 3: Join the two halves of lining together, make two rows of machine stitching along ½in seams of the shaped sides.

Step 4: Pin the lining inside the frame, stretch lining to give a smooth, tight fit. Keep side seams against side struts of frame.

Step 5: Draw lining over top and bottom rings of frame, matching scallops of lining to frame. Turn under raw edges and topstitch in place.

To make cover

Step 1: Using your brown paper pattern place it on the cross of the covering material. Cut out making it ¼in larger all round. Cut two halves.

Step 2: Join the two pieces together and fit over the frame, making sure that the seams correspond with the shaped side struts.

Step 3: Topstitch to the bottom ring keeping the scallops firmly in shape. Turn over raw edges at the top of the shade and sew to lining inside frame.

Step 4: Stitch decorative braid round top and bottom edges.

Tiffany Lampshade

A pretty lampshade which will add a bright decorative note to a room.

Material

You will need a frame of suitable size made of strong and non-springy wire. To cover the shade, choose a fabric with two-way stretch such as silk, shantung, linen, rayon, or cotton. Bind the top edge, bottom edge and two opposite struts of the frame with white tape so that you can sew the fabric to them. Cut the tape twice the length needed and tape the struts from top to bottom, turning and binding the tape away from you. Pull the tape as taut and as smooth as possible and tie and tuck in the ends. Tape the top, then the bottom. Stitch the final tape joints firmly.

To make

Step 1: Make a pattern of the frame in calico or part of an old sheet. Fold the fabric on the cross and pin to half the frame using the bound struts for pinning. Pin to top and bottom pulling the fabric taut as you do so.

Step 2: Fit the pattern on the half frame until it is free from puckers. With a pencil draw round the shape of the half frame, top, bottom and sides. Unpin from frame.

Step 3: Cut out pattern, cutting away from the lines.

Step 4: Fold lining for shade on the cross, soft, pliable material such as jersey is best to use.

Step 5: Place pattern on it and cut out two pieces of fabric.

Step 6: Pin lining together along the marked lines from pattern and stitch side seams. Place over frame, trim the seams and make sure they are in the centre of the two stays. Pull and pin the lining into place and firmly oversew it at top and bottom of the shade. Cut off excess fabric close to the stitching.

To make the cover: Fold the fabric on the cross and using your pattern cut out two pieces of fabric. Allow 1in all round for sewing and pinning. Pin one thickness of the fabric to the top and bottom end of each bound strut of half the shade. Smooth out

The drum lampshade is the simplest to make and one of the most versatile.

any creases and then pin out the rest of the fabric. Pencil mark the outer stays on the fabric, then take the fabric off the frame. Fit the two right sides of the fabric together, making sure you pin the second side to match the first. Machine the two pieces together.

Trim seams and ease the fabric into place over the frame. Pull and pin the fabric into place until there are no creases then firmly oversew it at top and bottom of the shade. Trim excess raw edges to ¼in and fold over to cover previous row of stitching then stitch down again.

For a final finish bias trim, fringe or decorative braid may be sewn along the bottom edge and along the top.

Making a Shaped Lampshade

When making fabric lampshades, it is necessary to bind the frame with tape. This not only makes a good finish inside the shade but also gives a firm foundation for sewing the cover.

To make

Step 1: Start binding top at a strut. Place one end of tape over and under the strut and back on top of the ring. Bind firmly with a slight overlap.

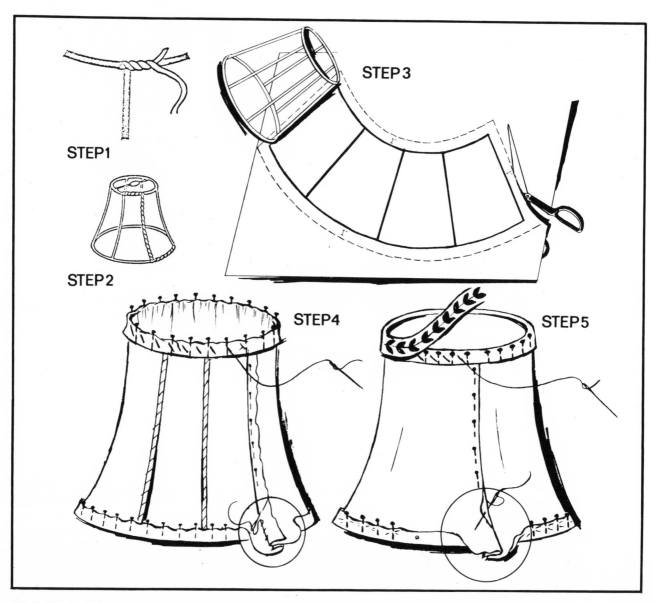

SHAPED LAMPSHADE

Step 2: Bind the frame tightly and smoothly in sections. Cut off tape and stitch firmly as you finish each section.

Step 3: Roll lampshade across a sheet of paper, marking the outline with a pencil. Cut out shape.

This gives you a pattern. Fold fabric on the bias. Cut out allowing 1in all round for seams. Cut a matching piece for the lining using the same seam allowance.

Step 4: Pin lining to inside of the bottom ring, drawing edges to the outside. Pull fabric up and over the top ring, stretch taut and pin any excess fabric into side seam. When lining is smooth, trim off excess fabric. Sew to the rings. Slip-stitch side seams with small, neat stitches.

Step 5: Pin outside cover part way round bottom ring, stretch to the top and pin in position. Continue pinning cover to the bottom ring then to the top ring. Pin seam. Trim off excess fabric and sew with raw edges outside. Blind stitch the side seam. Cover the raw edges with a braid trim. Either handsew the braid in place or use a colourless self adhesive specially made for fabrics.

This attractive scalloped lampshade brings colour interest to a room.

An elegant shaped lampshade.

Decorative braid is stitched round the top and bottom edges of this Tiffany lampshade.

Index